Lonely planet Kids

HOW TO BE A SPACE EXPLORER

YOUR OUT-OF-THIS-WORLD ADVENTURE

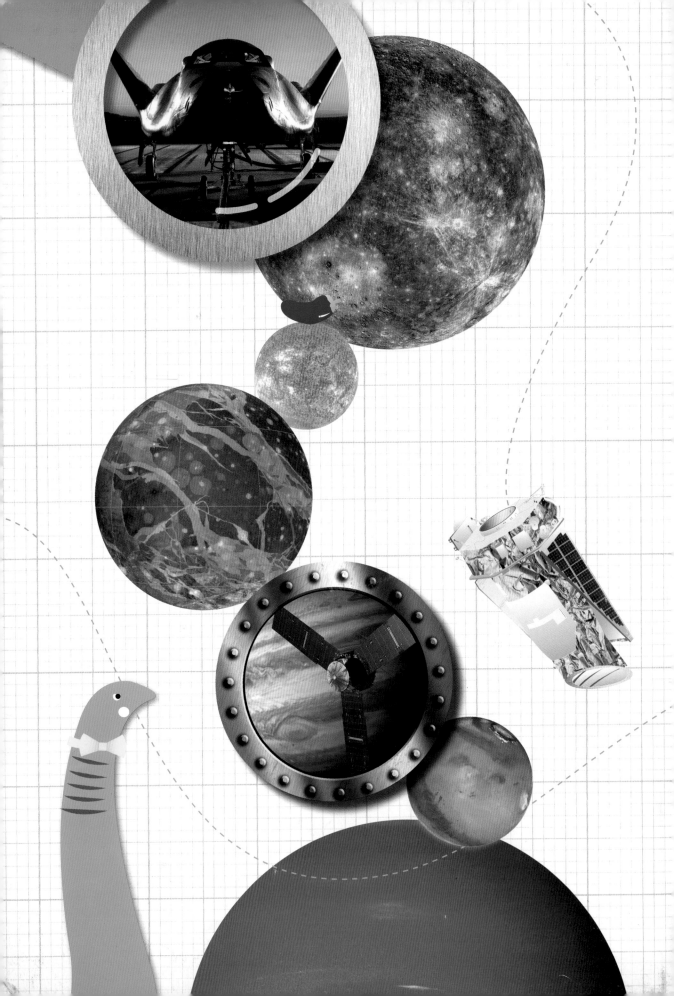

CONTENTS

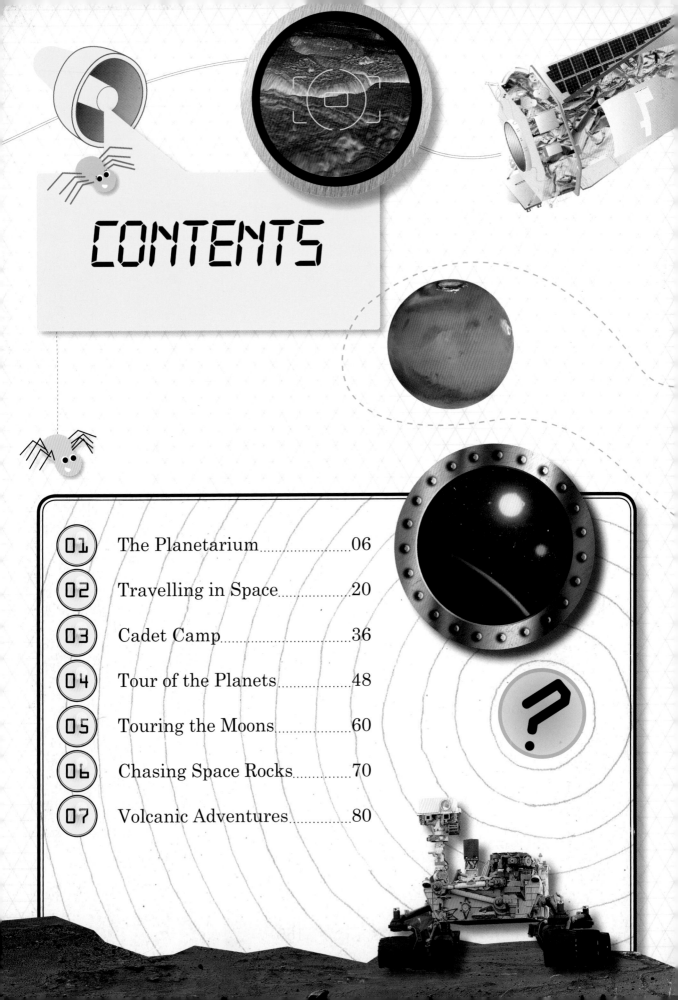

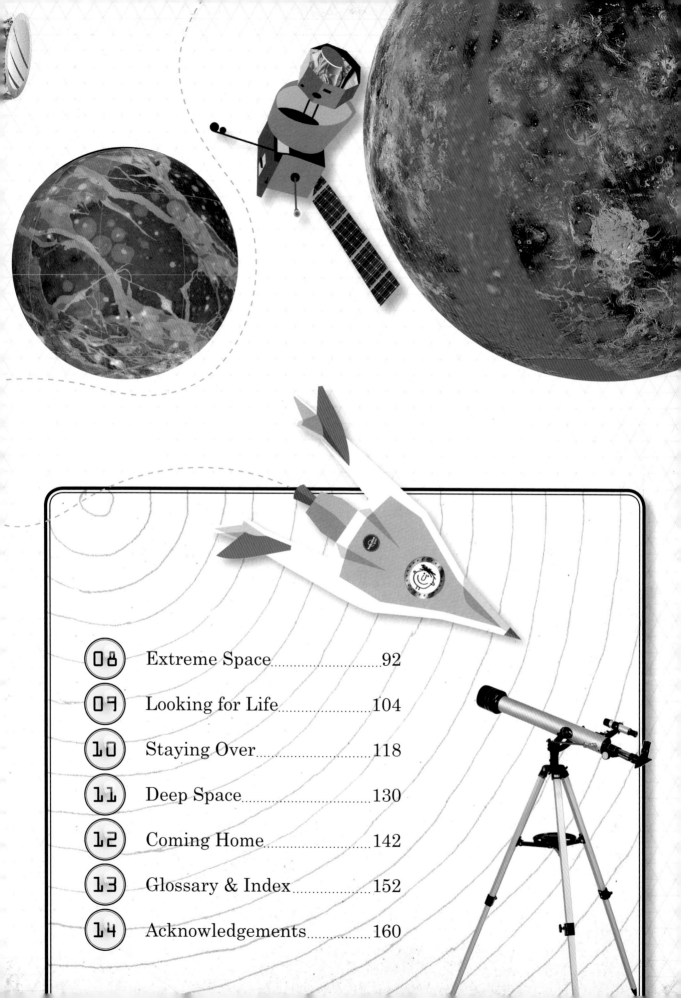

01 THE PLANETARIUM

There are many worlds to explore beyond this little planet we call home. Only recently, over the last 150 years or so, have we begun to find out what they might be like. Since the 1950s, we've been snooping around our Solar System. Astronauts have travelled in Earth's orbit and to the Moon, while robotic spacecraft (yes, robots!) have visited the Sun, its planets, and have delved into even deeper space.

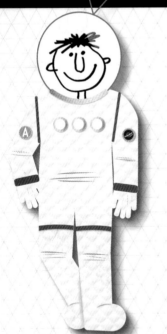

As a human, you have an urge to explore. To travel to new places, cross that canyon, climb that crater, or set foot on that new world. Out of the tens of thousands of people involved in space exploration – planning, researching and building spacecraft – only a few of those are lucky enough to actually travel into space.

Should you become one of those chosen few, this book will prepare you for the worlds beyond our planet.

IT'S TIME FOR YOU TO PLAY YOUR PART IN OUR CONQUEST OF SPACE.

WARNING!

Only the fearless need read on. Prepare to have your mind blown by the sheer size and scale of the Universe. Get your mind into cosmic gear!

Calling all space explorers, calling all space explorers...

Please report to the Planetarium. Your first assignment is the Solar System. You need to find out what it is, where it is, and how it fits into the overall scheme of the Universe.

ONLY 12 PEOPLE HAVE EVER SET FOOT ON ANOTHER WORLD (THE MOON).

Your training begins

Fasten your seat belts, space cadets, as we take you on the trip of a lifetime. The Known Universe is your destination, and the journey is about to begin. **You must prepare.**

Kit Checklist:

- ☐ A TELESCOPE OR PAIR OF BINOCULARS
- ☐ A RED NIGHT-VISION TORCH
- ☐ A COMPASS
- ☐ A NOTEPAD
- ☐ YOUR SPIRIT OF ADVENTURE
- ☐ AN OPEN MIND

OPERATION: TELESCOPE

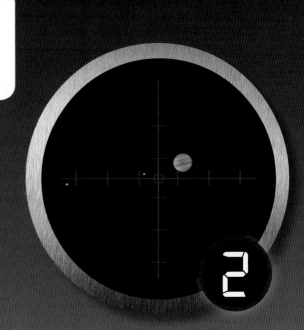

There's a whole Universe of incredible wonder out there. It's all above your head. It's your destination, so take a good look. But first, you'll need to gather up some important bits of kit to help you with your astronomical field trip.

1 THE MOON

The best views to be had of the Moon are close to the 'lunar terminator', the line that divides the sunlit portion of its surface from the unlit parts. Here you will notice the lunar craters, casting long, cool shadows when they are close to the terminator. These shadows make them easier to see.

2 THE PLANETS

The thick clouds of Venus are illuminated by the Sun, and the planet can often be seen just before sunrise or just after sunset. Jupiter and its moons are a lovely sight, too. Four of Jupiter's moons are planet-sized. If you can spot these 'Galilean' moons, look again two hours later. You may see that the moons have moved slightly.

3 COMETS AND METEORS

Comets travel on long journeys around the Sun, so we can only see them from Earth at certain times. As they approach the Sun, they grow twinkling 'tails' of dusty and gassy material. Meteor showers are a similar sight. In the northern hemisphere – the parts of the world above the equator – meteors are best seen in August and November.

COSMIC!

STARS

From the Earth, stars appear in chance patterns known as constellations. They're named after objects (such as the Plough), animals (such as the Chamaeleon) and characters from ancient myths (such as Orion). There are 88 recognised constellations in all, and it's really fun trying to spot some of them.

 GALAXIES

Our nearest large galaxy, Andromeda, can be seen in the Andromeda constellation. It appears to us as a stretched, fuzzy blob, and it is the farthest object we can see with the naked eye! It's 2.5 million light years away – this means the light from it has taken 2.5 million years to get to your eyes. So you're seeing Andromeda as it looked 2.5 million years ago.

SPECIAL BRIEFING: THE SUN

The first stop on your journey is the Sun. It's brilliant – in more ways than one. As you know, the Sun is way too hot to actually visit in person. You'd get scorched into oblivion. And it doesn't make any difference if you set off at night, when it's a bit cooler! The first thing you need to learn is that our Sun is the local star, and that stars are the most important building blocks in the Universe.

The Sun is the key to all life on our planet. Without the Sun there would be no light, no heat, no food, no weather, no days and no seasons. In fact, there would be no Solar System at all.

The Sun is a ball of fiery energy. Unbelievably, it burns about 4 million tonnes of gas every second. That's as much energy as seven trillion nuclear reactions occurring every second. Ouch! No wonder it's so hot!

ISOKM/H
93MPH

DISTANT STAR

The Sun is about 150 million kilometres (93 million miles) away from Earth. That's a fair trek. If you set your spacecraft to travel at a constant speed of 150km/h (93mph), it'll still take you a million hours to get there. That's an approximate journey time of 114 Earth years – on a one-way ticket!

SUN SIZE

You could fit more than a million Earths inside the Sun. To travel all the way around it in an expensive, heat-resistant spacecraft – travelling at roughly 800km/h (500mph) – you would need to keep going, non-stop, for 227 Earth days.

SUPER-HOT CORE

At its surface, the Sun has a temperature of about 5,500°C (9,900°F). But inside, it's really cooking, with a core temperature of about 15,000,000°C (60,000,000°F). One of the Sun's main jobs is making new atoms. It is an atom-making machine that lights up the entire Solar System with sunshine power.

STAR ENERGY

Space experts believe that the Sun has been doing its atom-making job for about five billion years. In all that time, it has been an energy-giving star, constantly sending out huge amounts of light and heat.

UNIVERSAL POWER

It's not just in our local system that sun-power is crucial. All the stars in the sky are suns, too. Many of them have planets in orbit about them. Stars power our entire Universe.

Our Solar System

Trainees – you now need to get familiar with the map of the Solar family. Our Solar System is made up of the Sun and all the bodies in orbit around it. These are the inner, 'rocky' planets nearest the Sun – Mercury, Venus, Earth and Mars – and the outer, 'gas giant' planets – Jupiter, Saturn, Uranus and Neptune.

Solar System Objects

This planetary system is also home to a belt of asteroids, which sits between Mars and Jupiter, and thousands of other small bodies, such as dwarf planets and comets. There's a lot to explore, so switch on your planetary data screens now.

Activity Panel: Spaced out

As you can see from the planetary data above, the distances between the planets of the Solar System are unbelievably huge. But using a roll of toilet paper can help you to imagine them. So, before leaving planet Earth, get yourself a roll of toilet paper with at least 100 sheets in it. Next, roll out the toilet roll in a long hallway, corridor or garden. Using a different pen colour for each one, mark off the position of the planets carefully – referring to your planetary data – to get a good idea of the distances between them.

MERCURY 1TPS	VENUS 2TPS	EARTH 2.5TPS	MARS 4TPS	JUPITER 13TPS	SATURN 24TPS	URANUS 48TPS	NEPTUNE 76TPS
ADS: 58M KM 36M Mi	ADS: 108M KM 67M Mi	ADS: 150M KM 93M Mi	ADS: 228M KM 142M Mi	ADS: 778M KM 483M Mi	ADS: 1427M KM 887M Mi	ADS: 2871M KM 1784M Mi	ADS: 4498M KM 2795M Mi
Orbit: 88 days	Orbit: 225 days	Orbit: 365 days	Orbit: 687 days	Orbit: 12 yrs	Orbit: 30 years	Orbit: 84 years	Orbit: 165 years
Size: 0.38xED	Size: 0.95xED	Size: 1xED	Size: 0.53xED	Size: 10.93xED	Size: 9xED	Size: 3.97xED	Size: 3.86xED
Moons: 0	Moons: 0	Moons: 1	Moons: 2	Moons: 67	Moons: 62	Moons: 27	Moons: 14

1   2   2.5   4   13   24   48   76

KEY

ADS: Average Distance from the Sun.

Orbit: the time it takes for the planet to orbit the Sun once, measured in Earth days.

Size: the diameter (or thickness) of each planet, compared with Earth's diameter of 12,756km (7926 miles).

TPS: Toilet Paper Sheets! Each Sun-to-planet distance when measured using standard sheets of toilet paper.

GRAVITY SIMULATOR

Step into the Gravity Simulator, strap yourself in and hold on tight. It's time to feel the full force of a young star – there's no better way to learn how the Solar System was created. There may be as many as 50 billion planets in our Galaxy alone. Now you can see exactly how they were formed.

GRAVITY

The fundamental force of gravity has played a major part in making our Universe the way it is. On our planet, it causes things to fall down, instead of up. But what exactly IS it?

Gravity is an invisible force of attraction between bodies that have mass. It is what makes bits of matter bunch together into stars, planets and moons. Gravity is what makes planets orbit their stars, like Earth orbits the Sun. And gravity is what makes cities of stars bunch together in huge, swirling galaxies.

YOUNG SUN

More the 4.5 billion years ago, clouds of particles started to drift together through the attractive force of gravity. Tens of millions of years later, this dense gathering of material was now glowing with heat and light. It had become a young star – our Sun.

BABY PLANETS

Around the young Sun, all this gassy and dusty material then formed itself into a swirling disc. The material was orbiting the star, because of the growing mass – and gravitational pull – of that central Sun. Gradually, tiny grains of gas and dust then collided and clumped together to make what astronomers call 'planetary embryos' – baby planets!

GROWING WORLDS

It's pretty cool to think that huge planets began their lives as tiny clumps, maybe only 200m (650ft) wide, which gradually stuck together to form young worlds. Scientists believe this is quite normal – and that's why they expect there to be lots and lots of planets out in the Universe.

Gravity Duvet

He said that gravity is what happens when space is curved or warped around a mass, such as a star or a planet. So a star or planet would cause a kind of 'dip' in space – so that any other object that came too near would tend to 'fall' into the dip.

Imagine your duvet is like space. What happens when you drop a heavy ball (your star or planet) onto the surface of your flat duvet? The duvet around the bowling ball dips, or bends. We say that something is 'massive' when it contains a lot of matter (stuff). The heavier – or more massive – your ball is, the bigger the dip will be in your space duvet.

SCIENTIST ALBERT EINSTEIN (1879–1955) HAD A GREAT IDEA ABOUT GRAVITY.

Light Year Simulator

Space is about 100km (62 miles) away. That sounds far, but in the grand scheme of things it isn't that far. If any of you trainees lived in – for example – Seattle, Canberra, Hyderabad, Cairo, Beijing or central Japan, space would be closer to you than the sea is. Distances across space, from object to object, are far greater – and here's where you start learning how to measure them.

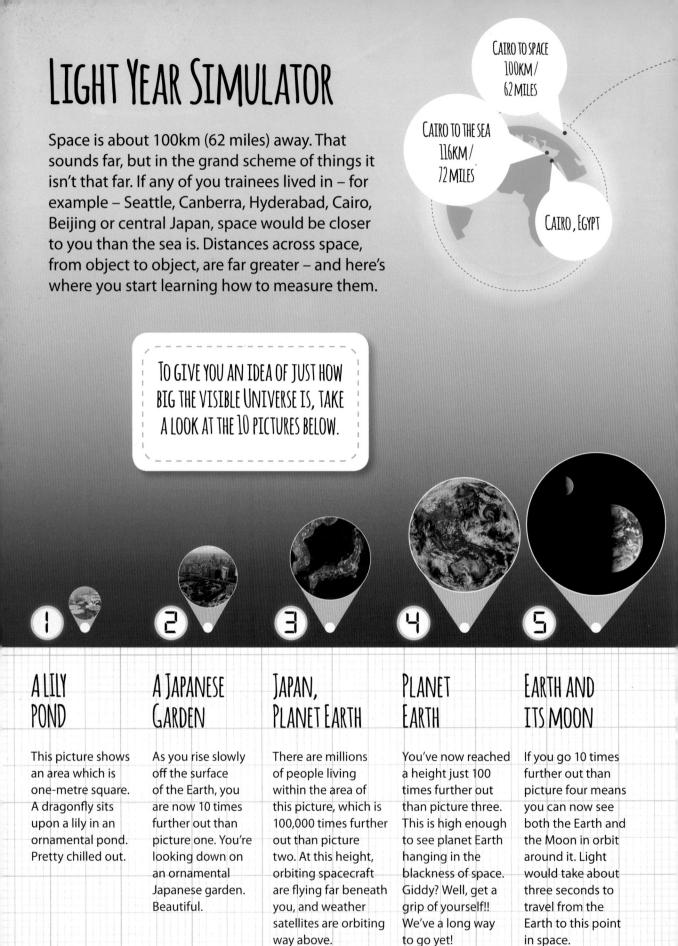

Cairo to space
100km /
62 miles

Cairo to the sea
116km /
72 miles

Cairo, Egypt

To give you an idea of just how big the visible Universe is, take a look at the 10 pictures below.

① A Lily Pond

This picture shows an area which is one-metre square. A dragonfly sits upon a lily in an ornamental pond. Pretty chilled out.

② A Japanese Garden

As you rise slowly off the surface of the Earth, you are now 10 times further out than picture one. You're looking down on an ornamental Japanese garden. Beautiful.

③ Japan, Planet Earth

There are millions of people living within the area of this picture, which is 100,000 times further out than picture two. At this height, orbiting spacecraft are flying far beneath you, and weather satellites are orbiting way above.

④ Planet Earth

You've now reached a height just 100 times further out than picture three. This is high enough to see planet Earth hanging in the blackness of space. Giddy? Well, get a grip of yourself!! We've a long way to go yet!

⑤ Earth and its Moon

If you go 10 times further out than picture four means you can now see both the Earth and the Moon in orbit around it. Light would take about three seconds to travel from the Earth to this point in space.

LIGHT YEARS

Space is vast. It's so huge, we need to use a special unit – called a light year – in order to measure it. One light year is the distance light travels in 365 Earth days. Light is the fastest thing known to us. A beam of light will travel at almost 300,000km (186,000 miles) in one second. This means it can travel about 10 trillion (that's 10 million million) kilometres, or 6 trillion miles, in a year.

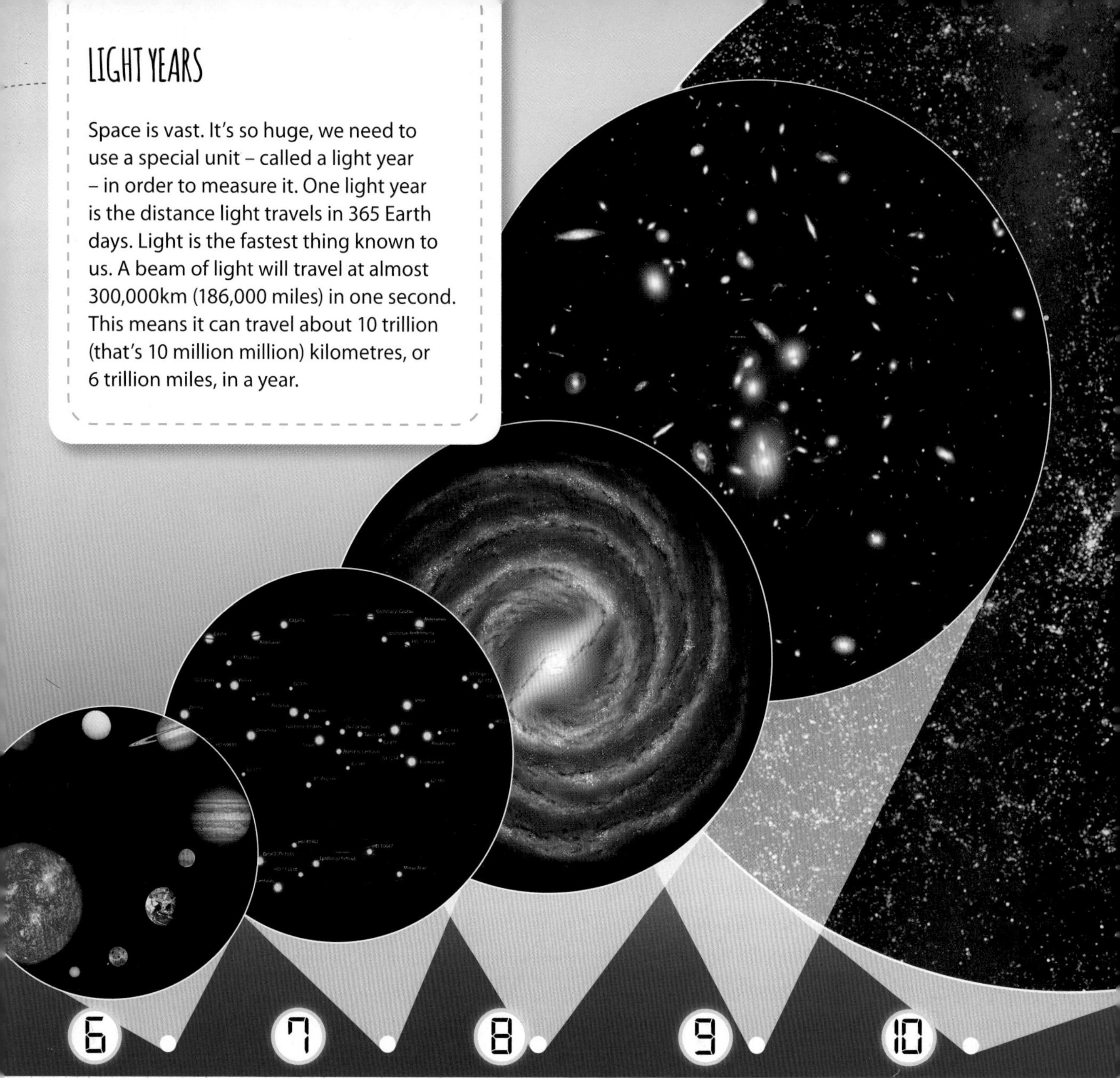

6

7

8

9

10

SOLAR SYSTEM

You are now so far from home that you can see the giant, gassy planets of the Solar System – Jupiter, Saturn, Uranus and Neptune – as they orbit the Sun. This is 10,000 times further out than picture five is, and it would take light about nine hours to get here.

SOLAR NEIGHBOURHOOD

You can now see the Sun at the very centre of this picture, as well as the very brightest of its neighbouring stars. You are now 10 light years away from home.

MILKY WAY GALAXY

Looking at this picture, you can see that the Sun is part of a vast Galaxy of stars, known as the Milky Way. This is more than 100,000 light years from planet Earth.

GALAXY CLUSTERS

But space doesn't end with the Milky Way. At the distance shown here, you can see that our Galaxy is joined by clusters of other galaxies, all moving through space. Light would take 100 million years to travel to this distance from Earth.

KNOWN UNIVERSE

Once you get about 10 billion light years away from our planet, you'll be able to see the whole of the visible Universe.

Light Years Away

You've learnt about light years, so now it's time to see exactly how far light has travelled through the Universe – and how long it takes to get from place to place. Lasers are very intense, focused beams of light. Using this laser-beam generator, you're going to travel – along with the light – to extremely distant parts of the cosmos.

HELLO, NEIGHBOUR! HELLO..? NEIGHBOUR?

Riding on a Beam

Travelling from Earth to the Moon, at light speed, would take you only one light second. If you blink, you'll miss it. From Earth to the Sun would take a whole 8.3 light minutes, and it would take you around 40 minutes to get to Jupiter, the largest planet in our system. Now, continue on our beam and head out to the stars.

The Sun's Neighbour

Proxima Centauri is the star that's nearest to the Sun. It is around 40 trillion km (25 trillion miles) away, which is about 4.24 light years.

PROXIMA CENTAURI
40 TRILLION KM / 25 TRILLION MILES

ANDROMEDA GALAXY
2,500,000 LIGHT YEARS

IS ANYBODY OUT THERE?

Width of a Galaxy

The diameter of the Milky Way Galaxy is somewhere between 100,000 and 120,000 light years. That means it would take you up to 120,000 years to travel across it on your super-fast beam of light. Gulp.

Billions of Galaxies

We reckon that the Universe – that's everything that exists in space – is made up of about 170 billion galaxies. Wow. The Milky Way's galactic neighbour is the Andromeda Galaxy, which is approximately 2.5 million light years from Earth. Galaxies of different types are grouped into clusters, and those clusters are found in vast regions of space known as superclusters.

Billions of Stars

Our Sun, along with Earth and the rest of the Solar System, orbits the centre of the Milky Way Galaxy. It travels on a 'spiral arm' – one of the many great regions of stars that extend out from the galactic centre. There are between 200 and 400 billion other stars orbiting, along with the Sun. They include solar neighbours such as Proxima Centauri (still no reply from there) and the supergiant star, Betelgeuse.

THE UNIVERSE IS ENORMOUS. THERE'S TOO MUCH TO EXPLORE! BUT YOU CAN AT LEAST EXPLORE LITTLE CHUNKS OF IT.

02 TRAVELLING IN SPACE

Before you can even think about setting foot on other worlds, you must first learn all about how you are going to actually get there. The idea of travelling into space is hundreds of years old. Until the middle of the 20th century, it remained in the realms of science fiction – but there are now many different ways of achieving it.

BE PATIENT, KEEP FOCUSED, AND YOU WILL SOON BE JETTING OUT INTO SPACE.

Orbit Calculator

Distance: 100
Speed   : 5mps
Gravity : 90%
Orbit   : 90 min
Velocity: 17,500
G-force : 20

8.5342719b4 47b8
9033 b57200 b472

Enter the Simulator

Now you know the sheer scale of space, and the huge distances that exist between objects. You will now learn how to travel to your chosen destination. You are about to discover the ways of rocketry, sail, and spacecraft.

BARF BAG

Kit Checklist:

☐ Training jumpsuit
☐ Sick bag
☐ Orbit calculator
☐ Hosepipe
☐ Bicycle pump
☐ Fizzy drink bottle

GRAVITATIONAL FORCES

Like the wind and sunlight on Earth, gravity is 'free energy'. Spacecraft can use it to orbit worlds, land on them, and slingshot past them to travel faster and further.

ONE IN THREE ASTRONAUTS GETS SPACE SICK, SO DON'T BE SURPRISED IF YOU FEEL A BIT GIDDY... YOU HAVE BEEN WARNED!

Escape Velocity

Space travel may involve rocket science, but it isn't necessarily the hardest thing in the world. You could get into space with a rocket the size of a telegraph pole, just by going quite fast and steering it upwards. All you need to do is achieve the right 'escape velocity' – the speed that an object needs to go in order to escape the Earth's gravitational pull on it.

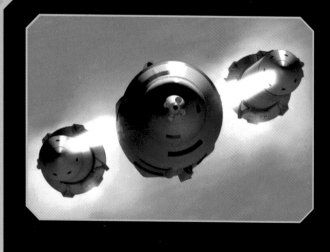

Escape From Earth

The escape velocity of a moon or planet depends on the strength of its gravitational pull. To get away from Earth, a rocket-powered spacecraft needs to reach a velocity of 11.2km (7 miles) per second. Achieving this often takes a lot of fuel, so some rockets are split into different 'stages' – each containing tanks of fuel – which fire one after another to propel a spacecraft or satellite into orbit.

Orbiting Earth

Crossing the 100km (62 miles) into space is easy enough. The trick is staying up there. There are several things you need to learn if you're going to achieve a good, steady orbital path around Earth – or around any other world, for that matter.

Low-Earth Orbiting

The International Space Station (ISS) is an example of a large satellite that travels around the world. The pull of gravity here is almost as strong as it is on the Earth's surface. The ISS hasn't actually escaped Earth's gravity, because it's still feeling about 90 per cent of the gravity we experience on the ground.

Orbital Speeds

To stop yourself – and your spacecraft – from falling back to the Earth, you have to travel along your orbital path really, really quickly. To stay locked on your orbit you need to set the craft's speed controls at about 8km (5 miles) per second.

ORBITAL OBSERVATION

You can study some orbital speeds from the ground. When you look at the sky at sunset, sometimes you'll see the ISS flying overhead. If you look again, 90 minutes later, you'll see it in the sky again. That's because, in those 90 minutes, the ISS has circled the entire world. In the movies or on TV, it may not look as if the astronauts are flying all that fast above the Earth – but in reality, the ISS would cross the length of a football field before a bullet had gone 9m (30ft). It's moving at 28,164km (17,500 miles) per hour.

TRY CATCHING THAT!

28 164

Rockets

As you have already begun your training as a space explorer, you will know that a rocket is a tall, cylinder-shaped vehicle that can be launched into space. The word 'rocket' can also mean a type of engine, as well as the vehicle that uses that engine.

1. Gas gets forced out

2. The rocket is pushed forwards

Rocket Engines

Like most engines, rockets work by burning fuel. The rocket engines convert the fuel into gas. The engine pushes the gas out of its back end, and this is what creates the 'propulsion' that moves the rocket in a certain direction. But don't be fooled – a rocket is not the same as the jet engine you'd find in an aircraft.

CREATING PROPULSION

Propulsion is the force by which something – such as a ship, a car or a space rocket – is moved forwards. A rocket is propelled (forced in a certain direction) using slow-burning gas, which escapes through a nozzle (the narrow, back end of a rocket). This generates a large amount of thrust and pushes the rocket upwards.

CHINESE ROCKET MAN

Moons ago lived a man named Wan Hu, an official of the Ming Dynasty. Early in the 1500s, Wan became the world's first astronaut. Making use of China's firework technology, Wan built his spaceship... a chair with 47 rockets attached to it. On launch day, Wan climbed onto his rocket chair. 47 assistants lit the 47 fuses, and ran for cover. There was a tremendous roar, and a huge explosion. The smoke cleared. The rocket chair was gone. Wan was never seen again.

Types of Fuel

A jet engine needs air to work, while a rocket engine does not. A rocket engine is designed to operate in the vacuum of space, where there is no air. There are two main types of rockets: liquid-fuel rockets and solid-fuel rockets.

SOYUZ

Liquid-fuel Rockets

The Russian Soyuz spacecraft are carried into space by rockets that use a liquid fuel. The National Aeronautics and Space Administration's (NASA) space shuttles (which were retired in 2011) carried a very large external fuel tank to power their engines. This tank was then detached as the shuttle's orbiter reached the edge of space.

Solid-fuel Rockets

You'll find solid fuels in fireworks and model rockets. Some space rockets use this kind of fuel as well. Lots and lots of it. The space shuttle also used solid fuel in its detachable Solid Rocket Boosters (SRBs) to help it get into orbit. Once they had fallen off, they could be reclaimed and reused in later flights.

ROCKET TEST

The mechanics of rocket science are so complicated, and expensive, that only a few nations have managed to launch people into orbit. When the Chinese put Yang Liwei in space, in 2003, they became only the third country to achieve this feat on their own. However, in theoretical terms, rockets are really rather simple. So simple, in fact, that you could build your own. It's time for some practical training.

IN THRUST WE TRUST!

It's time for your rocket training. Here are some reaction engines that you could try:

ROCKET HOSE

Turn on a water hose, full blast. As you hold the hose, you'll notice that it's acting like a rocket engine. The water is travelling in one direction, and the hose is pushing back in the opposite direction. What you're feeling is the 'reaction' force.

#1

#2

IF YOU DON'T HOLD THE HOSE FIRMLY, IT'LL THRASH AROUND AND MAKE A TREMENDOUS MESS. AND THEN YOU'LL BE IN TROUBLE WITH YOUR TRAINING OFFICER...

BALLOON THRUST

Blow up a balloon. Now let go. It flies around the room until it runs out of air. It's releasing gas – the air that you blew into it – just like a rocket does. When air thrusts out of the nozzle, or neck, of the balloon, the balloon reacts in the opposite direction. It's a mini-rocket!

Reaction Engines

Rocket engines are 'reaction' engines. As gases come out of the nozzle end of the rocket, the rocket itself reacts by being pushed upwards.

To every action, there is an equal and opposite reaction.

Sir Isaac Newton
1643-1727

In the case of the rocket, it works like this: the action is the gas coming out, the reaction is the rocket being thrust upwards. **Simple!**

#3

Bottle Rocket

1. Take an empty plastic bottle.

2. Partially fill the bottle with water. Seal it with a stopper that has a plastic pipe running through it.

3. Angle the bottle rocket so that its neck is pointing towards the ground.

4. Standing well out of the way, use a bicycle pump, or air compressor, to force air into the bottle through the pipe.

As you pump in the air, the pressure builds inside the bottle, and pushes water out of the only escape route – the narrow neck of the bottle. As with a rocket nozzle, the bottle's neck makes the thrust larger by forcing the water through a small space.

Fire your water rocket upwards, by pointing its nozzle towards the floor. You'll notice the rocket gets faster as it takes off. The thrust created by the escaping water is greater than both the resistance of the air around it and the weight of the rocket. So, as its weight gets less, the rocket will get faster until it runs out of water fuel.

Try your rocket flights several times, using different amounts of fuel. See how high you can get your rocket, and record your test flights! Some home-made rockets can reach speeds of 200km/h (124mph). The world-record height is more than 300m (almost 1000ft).

Can you beat the home-made rocket world-record...?! Remember to be careful with your aim...

Highest-reaching home-made rocket

Spacecraft Showroom

Spacecraft are vehicles designed to travel in space. They can be used for a number of tasks, including carrying humans and cargo, for Earth observation and communications, as well as planetary exploration. When planning a space mission to a destination, space agencies have a range of craft to choose from.

CHOOSING YOUR CRAFT:

The type of craft you choose, when planning your mission depends upon the kind of work you'll have to carry out. Whether or not you plan to put a human crew on board will also make a huge difference. Here are some options you might like to consider.

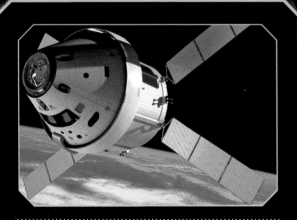

COMMAND AND SERVICE MODULES

These form the main part of the spacecraft and are designed to take people on trips beyond Earth's orbit. The service module holds life-support systems, providing water and air, and carries the fuel to power the spacecraft's engines. The command module is your mobile home, in which you'll control the craft through the onboard computer and navigation systems.

EXCURSION MODULES

Excursion modules, or landing modules, take people onto the surface of another world. The Lunar Excursion Module (LEM) did this, by enabling the Apollo astronauts to travel from their command module to the Moon from 1969-72. Such modules detach from the rest of the craft when in orbit around a planet or moon, and have different engines for descent (landing) and ascent (taking off again).

DETACHABLE PROBES

Space probes are designed to fall through a planet's atmosphere and make scientific studies of the conditions – either in the atmosphere itself, or on the planet's surface, or both. These vehicles need to be able to carry scientific instruments and high-resolution cameras. A very good example is the Huygens entry probe that landed on Saturn's moon Titan in 2005 (see pages 66–67).

ORBITERS

As their name suggests, orbiters – or motherships – are spacecraft that travel in orbit around the planet or moon they are studying. Some orbiters carry astronauts on board, while others are robotic. The space shuttle's orbiter was designed for crewed missions in Earth's orbit. There are many robotic orbiters that have been sent to study other worlds, such as Mars.

STATION-TO-GROUND MODULES

These modules are designed to be able to 'dock' with space stations and other spacecraft, and then 'detach' and return to Earth. The famous Russian Soyuz craft have been doing this since 1957, with over 1500 launches. Soyuz capsules are now used to transport people and supplies to and from the ISS.

> ROCKETS ARE USED TO LAUNCH OTHER SPACECRAFT MODULES INTO ORBIT. THE AMOUNT OF WEIGHT A ROCKET CAN CARRY IS KNOWN AS THE PAYLOAD. A PAYLOAD MAY INCLUDE CARGO, EXPERIMENTS AND PASSENGERS, AS WELL AS OTHER SPACECRAFT OR SPACE STATION MODULES.

A

SAILS AND ELEVATORS

Rockets are used to launch spacecraft, satellites, modules, ISS supplies and humans into orbit – and they enabled us to put astronauts on the Moon. Today, people are in orbit around the planet at all times. In order to travel into deeper space, you will need to look at all the different hi-tech options available to you.

SOLAR PANELS

STORAGE PROBLEMS

As any technician planning a human mission to Mars will tell you, using solid and liquid fuels for the journey is going to pose a major problem. Tonnes and tonnes of liquid fuel, for example, would be needed to get there. This would be very expensive, and designing a spacecraft that could store this fuel – and bear the weight of it when being launched – would be extremely challenging.

SOLAR POWER

The light energy given out by the Sun is already used to power the systems on board space station modules, satellites and robotic spacecraft. Their solar panels convert this energy into electrical power. There is no doubt that we will need to use solar energy to support the computers and life-support systems on humans missions to other worlds. It's unlikely, however, that enough power could be generated to fuel a spacecraft's engines.

Space Elevators

Imagine jumping into an elevator and pressing a button marked 'space station'. These space elevators would run on 47,000km-long (30,000 mile-long) cables made of carbon-based 'ribbons', 30 times stronger than steel. The elevator would use specially designed grips and rollers to move up and down the cables. Lasers, beamed up from Earth, would be converted into electrical energy for the cable car.

Space elevators were first imagined in an 1895 book called 'Daydreams of Heaven and Earth', by Russian rocket pioneer Konstantin Tsiolkovsky.

Solar Sailing

Sunlight contains particles of energy called photons. When these photons connect with an object – such as a wide solar sail – they each add a tiny amount of pressure. There's no air resistance in space. So, when the pressure from billions of tiny protons is added together, a small spacecraft could potentially be propelled through space.

Antimatter Engines

So, how do we solve your fuel storage problems for deep-space travel? Antimatter is a possible solution. Tiny antimatter particles behave in the opposite way to the kind of particles that make up 'normal' matter. So, when antimatter meets 'normal' matter, both break down in a great flash of energy. This energy – created by much smaller amounts of fuel – could be harnessed to power your spacecraft.

Descent And Landing

How you land on another world very much depends on the characteristics of that world. A moon or planet's make-up and gravity will have a big effect on your approach. This includes your spacecraft's entry and descent through the atmosphere, as well as how it touches down on the surface. Space experts call this the spacecraft's EDL – entry, descent and landing.

As your spacecraft hurtles through the atmosphere of a planet or moon, it will rub against its particles. This creates lots of friction, which results in high levels of heat. So your spacecraft needs to have special plates that can resist the extremely high temperatures of atmospheric entry.

PARACHUTES

Take Mars, for example. The red planet's atmosphere is one per cent as thick as the Earth's, and Martian gravity is one-third what you feel on Earth. If you're using a parachute to aid your descent, it needs to be able to create enough 'drag', or resistance, to slow your craft as it passes through this thin atmosphere. It also needs to be strong enough not to rip and tear during the descent. Make sure the design is right, and you will touch down safely!

THRUSTERS

Even though robotic explorers have been going to Mars for decades, the journey remains dangerous for every rover, probe and lander that makes it. About two-thirds of all Mars missions have failed. To help with your landing, 'retro rockets' – or reverse thrusters – could be used to steer your craft for a slower, softer and safer landing, without crashing!

AIRBAGS

Airbags may be used to 'bounce and roll' your craft to a safer landing. The gas-filled bags are designed to inflate – very rapidly – just before the parachutes are detached and the spacecraft impacts with the surface. For Mars missions, the airbags have to be sturdy enough to cushion the spacecraft if it landed on rocks or rough ground. They also need to allow the craft to bounce along the surface at speeds around 100km/h (62mph) after landing.

Landing And Roving

Rocky planets are great targets for exploration and, perhaps, colonisation. But when you land on them, you'll soon realise there is an awful lot of terrain (ground) to cover – even if you are planning to land at a specific site, for a particular reason. You may have been asked to sample and test the soil and rocks in that area. Walking around in weaker gravity can be a slow process – so it might be good to pack some wheels!

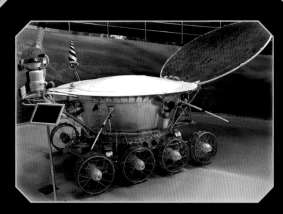

RUSSIAN ROVERS

Lunokhod 1 was the first successful rover, used by the Russians to explore the surface of the Moon, late in 1970. This 2.3m-long (7ft 7in-long) robotic vehicle was powered by batteries, which were recharged during the lunar day by a solar cell mounted on the underside of its lid. The cell converted the Sun's light energy into electrical energy.

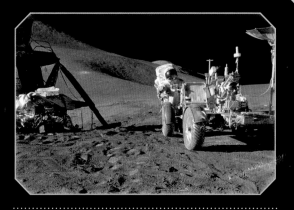

LUNAR ROVING VEHICLES

Perhaps the coolest rovers of all! NASA's Lunar Roving Vehicles (LRVs), also known as a 'Moon buggies', were battery-powered vehicles driven by US astronauts during the final three Apollo missions (Apollo 15, 16 and 17). The buggies were 'flat-packed' so that they could be stowed on the side of the lunar excursion module (see pages 28–29). All three LRVs remain on the Moon.

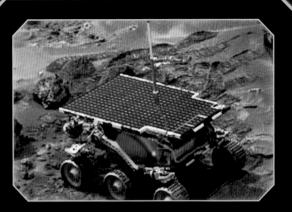

SOJOURNER

The Sojourner rover was part of NASA's Pathfinder mission to Mars in 1997. The uncrewed, remotely controlled rover analysed the Martian rocks and atmosphere, and was about the same size as a microwave oven. The rover was powered by solar panels and a non-rechargeable battery, which allowed it to perform limited night-time tasks. It was the data from this rover that led us to believe that Mars was once much 'wetter' in the past.

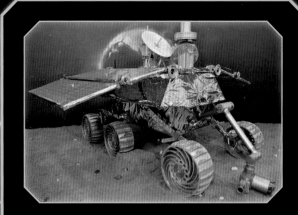

YUTU

Yutu was China's first lunar rover. It landed on the Moon in December 2013. Energy was provided by two solar panels, which allowed Yutu to do tasks in the lunar daytime. During the 14-day lunar nights, Yutu went into sleep mode.

SCARAB

A new type of lunar rover has been designed by NASA, to help astronauts carry rock samples and explore the Moon's surface. Amazingly, Scarab is also able to work on its own, covering some of the dark polar craters on the Moon, while you busy yourself doing kangaroo-hops in one-sixth of Earth's gravity.

Before designing your own, please wander around this showroom of roving vehicles – and study this brief history of robotic, interplanetary rovers! They have provided us with some of our most valuable data about the Moon and Mars.

03 CADET CAMP

All seasoned travellers are well prepared, and that includes space explorers. But how should the daring adventurer be equipped to climb a lunar crater or set foot on a more distant world? It's time to go to space-cadet training camp, where you will find out what it's like to be launched into space and live there for long periods of time. You'll also learn how to cope with long-haul space travel, landing on other worlds and exploring them.

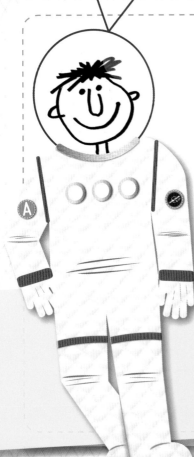

EVERY YEAR, SPACE AGENCIES SUCH AS NASA RECEIVE MANY THOUSANDS OF APPLICATIONS FROM PEOPLE WHO WANT TO BECOME ASTRONAUTS — SOMETIMES MORE THAN 6000. ONLY A HANDFUL OF THOSE PEOPLE WILL GET TO TRAVEL INTO SPACE ANY TIME SOON. SO YOU'LL HAVE TO BE PATIENT — BUT YOU MUST ALSO KEEP BELIEVING!

YOUR TRAINING GETS REAL

Members of the public can now sign up to a real-life 'Astronaut Training Experience' at visitor centres such as the Kennedy Space Centre in Florida, USA.

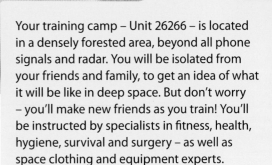

Your training camp – Unit 26266 – is located in a densely forested area, beyond all phone signals and radar. You will be isolated from your friends and family, to get an idea of what it will be like in deep space. But don't worry – you'll make new friends as you train! You'll be instructed by specialists in fitness, health, hygiene, survival and surgery – as well as space clothing and equipment experts.

Kit Checklist:

- ☐ Application form
- ☐ Map to secret location
- ☐ Spaceflight history books
- ☐ Virtual reality headset
- ☐ Extra-vehicular mobility unit (EMU)
- ☐ Lunar surface training suit

THE HISTORY OF SPACEFLIGHT

[TOP SECRET MISSION] ⚠

Joining instructions will be sent to you. Once you have absorbed the data, please destroy the details.

The Big Space Challenge

In the icy parts of our world, simply stepping outdoors is an adventure. You have to 'suit up' with thermal tops, trousers, underwear, coat, gloves, hat, scarf and boots. It's hard work just thinking about it! Getting dressed for going outside in space, or on another world, is a much more serious business. Extraterrestrial environments are the most extreme places that humans have ever faced.

CADET BRIEFING #1:
SPACEWALKING

In this training session, you'll hear about an explorer's essentials for surviving in space – not just when floating around on a spacewalk, but also when trundling about on the planets and moons of the Solar System.

Space is a hostile place. Your spacecraft will be specially pressurized, so that the air around you feels similar to how it does on an aircraft, for example. But space is a vacuum – there is no air there at all. If you were to step outside your spacecraft without a special suit on, the following things would happen:

Without oxygen to breathe, you'd pass out within about 15 seconds.

Because there is no air pressure, your blood and other body fluids could 'boil', and then freeze.

Your tissues – such as your skin, heart and other organs – could expand because of the boiling blood.

You would meet extreme temperature swings: in sunlight, temperatures in space can reach 120°C (248°F), and in the shade they may fall to -100°C (-148°F).

You would be exposed to dangerous levels of radiation, such as the solar wind (particles shooting out from the Sun) and cosmic radiation from distant galaxies.

Micro-meteoroids, travelling at high speeds, could hit your body like tiny bullets.

WATCH OUT FOR THOSE MICRO-METEOROIDS! THESE TINY PIECES OF SPACE DUST AND DEBRIS ARE ALMOST INVISIBLE, BUT THEY TRAVEL AT HIGH ENOUGH SPEEDS TO DO SERIOUS DAMAGE!

CADET BRIEFING #2:
PROTECTIVE CLOTHING

A well-designed, well-manufactured space suit can protect you from many of the dangers you will encounter in space and on other worlds, where the conditions are very different to those on Earth. Here are the main benefits of a good suit:

Space suits act as a 'personal spacecraft'. They create a pressurized atmosphere, inside the suit, to stop your blood boiling.

A space suit's life-support system supplies you with oxygen and removes the carbon dioxide you breathe. This prevents you from suffocating.

Water is circulated around the suit inside a special cooling garment. The water is cooled to keep you at a comfortable temperature when you are working and moving around, either in space or on other worlds.

The outer 'soft suit' has around 15 different layers. These protect your body from contact with space junk, micro-meteoroids and radiation.

Space suits are created in different segments, which fit together, to allow free movement and maximum comfort.

The suit's helmet normally has a gold-tinted visor, to protect human eyes from intense sunlight and dazzling reflections off other objects.

Now that you have seen the benefits of wearing a well-made suit, you can begin to choose the right materials and design your own suit on pages 42–43.

Learn from the Legends

Today's space suits are very sophisticated pieces of kit. It took a lot of research, planning and testing to arrive at the kind of suits that astronauts wear today. In this lesson, you can retrace the steps that astronauts had to take in order to find out how their bodies would react to being in space – and what kind of protective clothing they would therefore need.

The Jet Set

When jets first took off, in the late 1930s and 1940s, pilots needed to wear flight suits to cope with the lack of oxygen high up in the Earth's atmosphere. The suits provided breathable air if the jet cabin suddenly lost pressure. They were made of a fabric that could inflate like a balloon, with the pilots being fed oxygen through hoses.

PROFILE:
ERICH WARSITZ

Erich Warsitz (1906–83) was a German test pilot. In 1939, he became the first person to fly a turbo-jet aircraft. In the same year, he was also the first person to fly an aircraft fuelled and powered like a rocket.

The Mercury Suits

NASA's Mercury missions of 1959–63 used space suits. They were like jet pilot suits, but had laced boots, gloves and a helmet attached to the suit by a metal collar ring. The astronauts found it hard to move in the suit, as it was not designed for spacewalking. The suits looked metallic, as they had an aluminium layer on top of the suit's fabric.

THE ENTIRE APOLLO SUIT, INCLUDING BACKPACK, WEIGHED 82KG (180LB) ON EARTH, BUT ONLY 14KG (30LB) ON THE MOON, WHICH HAS ONLY ONE-SIXTH OF THE EARTH'S GRAVITY.

John Glenn (born in 1921) was the first American to orbit the Earth. In 1962, he circled the Earth three times in his Friendship 7 space capsule. In 1998, he flew on board the space shuttle Discovery.

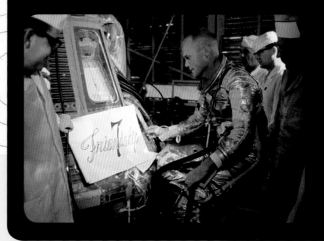

ASTRONAUTS ON SOCIAL MEDIA

In the modern age, we can communicate with astronauts and ask them questions via the internet and social media websites. This has turned regular astronauts into very famous people! Commander Chris Hadfield, a Canadian astronaut, became a household name in 2013 after he played guitar and sang a rock song on board the International Space Station. The video of his performance has been viewed on the internet by millions of people.

PROFILE:
NEIL ARMSTRONG

Neil Armstrong (1930–2012) was the first human being to set foot on the Moon. Along with Edwin 'Buzz' Aldrin, he touched down on the lunar surface inside the Eagle landing module on 20 July 1969.

Your Space Suit

Imagine the scene… You've launched off from Earth, you're now in the planet's orbit and you're getting ready to perform your very first spacewalk. What exactly should you wear for your Extra-vehicular Activity (EVA) and what sort of materials are going to protect your body from harm while allowing you to move around freely?

THESE PRICEY SUITS CATER FOR YOUR EVERY NEED; YOU CAN EVEN PEE IN THEM! THE SUITS HAVE A NAPPY LAYER, CALLED A MAG (MAXIMUM ABSORPTION GARMENT), WHICH ALLOWS THE ASTRONAUT TO URINATE AT WILL, STRAIGHT INTO THE MAG. LUXURY!

EACH EMU SUIT COSTS **£7 MILLION ($12 MILLION)**

IT'S JUST AS WELL THE SPACE AGENCY IS PAYING, AS THAT AMOUNT WOULD SURELY BREAK YOUR PIGGY BANK. SO WHEN YOU WEAR IT, LOOK AFTER IT. SPACE SUITS COST THE EARTH!

EMU SUITS

The first space suits were tailored for each astronaut. The EMU comes in components (segments) of varying sizes, so they can be put together to fit any astronaut – including you!

It sounds like you'll be dressing up to look like a bird – but, in fact, 'EMU' stands for extra-vehicular mobility unit. That's a posh way of saying 'suit-for-moving-about-outside-a-spacecraft'. Early space suits were made of soft fabrics, but today's EMU is far tougher. The soft parts of the suit contain up to 15 layers of material: first, you need to put on an inner, liquid-cooling garment (two layers), then a pressure garment (two layers), then a thermal micro-meteoroid garment (eight layers). On top of all of this lies an outer cover (one layer).

EMU MATERIALS

Your space suit will be made from the finest modern, artificial materials. Some of these will already be familiar to you…

- **Nylon tricot:** also used as a lining material in suitcases.
- **Spandex:** a light, stretchy material also worn by athletes.
- **Urethane-coated Nylon**
- **Dacron:** also used to make violin bows.
- **Neoprene-coated Nylon**
- **Mylar:** also used to make the foil-like lids for dairy goods such as yoghurt.
- **Gortex:** a very common, waterproof fabric used to make hiking boots, jackets and so on.
- **Kevlar:** a super-tough material found in bullet-proof vests.
- **Nomex:** used to make the flame-proof jumpsuits that racing drivers wear.

A modern EMU is made up of the following parts:

1 **Maximum Absorption Garment (MAG)**
collects your pee when nature calls.

2 **Liquid Cooling and Ventilation Garment (LCVG)**
takes away excess body heat.

3 **EMU Electrical Harness (EEH)**
links up the communications devices and bio-instruments (which measure how your body is doing).

4 **Communications Carrier Assembly (CCA)**
contains microphones and earphones that are used for communications.

5 **Lower Torso Assembly (LTA)**
includes pants, knee and ankle joints, boots and lower waist segments.

6 **Hard Upper Torso (HUT)**
has a hard shell that supports the arms, torso (upper body), helmet, backpack and control module.

7 **Arm segments**

8 **Gloves, outer and inner**
are heated, to aid the movement of the fingers while doing jobs outside the spacecraft.

9 **Helmet**

10 **Extravehicular Visor Assembly (EVA)**
protects the astronaut's face and eyes from bright sunlight.

11 **In-suit Drink Bag (IDB)**
provides drinking water during spacewalks.

12 **Primary Life Support Subsystem (PLSS)**
supplies cooling water, oxygen, power, radio and a warnings system, and removes poisonous carbon dioxide.

13 **Secondary Oxygen Pack (SOP)**
is there just in case the main supply runs out.

14 **Display and Control Module (DCM)**
operates the PLSS.

Simulation Training

Your physical astronaut training will get you ready for two main things: stuff relating to the spacesuits, and stuff relating to the actual experience of being and working in space. So, next up is your space experience: how to cope with weightlessness, spatial disorientation – in other words, totally losing your sense of direction – and motion sickness.

Space training is a whole-body workout. You need to know how your body is going to react to being in space – and whether it is fit enough.

VIRTUAL REALITY

Technical training happens in the Virtual Reality (VR) labs. They will prepare you for spacewalks and robotic arm work. In orbit, you might need to work with the robotic arm attached to the ISS, to fix machinery such as a space telescope, a satellite or the modules of the space station itself. The lab uses powerful computers, special gloves, a video display helmet, a chest pack and a controller. The VR tests will also teach you to find your direction when moving around in space.

BUOYANCY LABS

Weightlessness training takes place in giant swimming pools called 'neutral buoyancy labs'. The labs simulate the low gravity of space, and the pools hold around 25 million litres of water! Deep in the pool, you will be trained for your spacewalks. To pass the tests, you'll need to spend 10 hours underwater for every hour you plan to spend walking in space.

SWIM TESTS

First up, swimming. Test One is to swim, non-stop, three lengths of a 25m pool. In Test Two, you now have to swim three lengths of the pool in a flight suit and tennis shoes, with no time limit. Test Three is to tread water for 10 minutes, wearing your flight suit. To complete the training, you also need to be able to scuba-dive, which means swimming underwater using a breathing set.

I HOPE YOU ENJOY STUDYING! ALL ASTRONAUT TRAINEES NEED TO BURY THEIR HEADS IN STUDIES OF SPACECRAFT, GEOLOGY, WEATHER SYSTEMS AND ASTRONOMY – AS WELL AS THEIR OWN MISSION OBJECTIVES.

THE VOMIT COMET

As an astronaut trainee, you'll also need to take a ride on the Vomit Comet, also known as a 'reduced gravity aircraft'. The plane is flown to a great height, where the engine is cut off. As the aircraft goes into a slow free-fall, towards the ground, the trainees on board experience weightless conditions for about 25 seconds. Be warned – you'll soon know how the aircraft got its nickname!

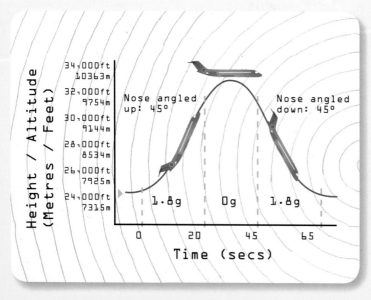

Height / Altitude (Metres / Feet)

34,000ft 10363m
32,000ft 9754m
30,000ft 9144m
28,000ft 8534m
26,000ft 7925m
24,000ft 7315m

Nose angled up: 45°

Nose angled down: 45°

1.8g   0g   1.8g

0   20   45   65

Time (secs)

Boot Camp on the Moon

To complete your training, the last set of tests will take place on the Moon. On your journey to the lunar surface you will experience a real rocket launch, you will dock with another spacecraft in the Earth's orbit, and you will learn how to land and work on the Moon itself. This is one giant step for a space explorer!

Journey to the Moon

The main stages of lift-off, from Earth, are automatic – so let the technology take the strain. The first two stages of your rocket (see pages 22–23) fall away – once they have used up their fuel – and soon you're travelling at 30,000km/h (18,500mph). As the third and final stage falls away, you head for the Moon in your Command and Service Module (CSM). You can now engage the CSM engines to navigate towards a lunar orbit (around the Moon).

Lessons From the 1960s

The NASA missions of the 1960s (see pages 28–29) were designed to put people on the Moon – and in doing so they taught us how to do some very complicated things in space. The Apollo astronauts had to use their Command and Service Module (CSM) to extract their landing vehicle (the LEM) from the final stage of the launch rocket. They also needed to be able to dock with the LEM once more, in a lunar orbit, so that the Moon astronauts could re-join and crawl back into the CSM, for the trip back home!

Lunar Landing

Once your CSM has detached the third rocket stage, and you're in orbit about the Moon, the next step is to crawl into your landing module. This should now be attached to the front end of your CSM. Once inside, with the hatches sealed, you can detach and begin your descent to the lunar surface. Your training camp is based at the Sea of Tranquility – famous for being the site of the very first Moon landing, made by the Apollo 11 astronauts.

Lunar Surface Training

The Moon's surface is a great place to practise moving around and working in a completely alien environment. As you know, its gravity is only one-sixth that of Earth's, so you need to learn how to move around in a different way. The best technique is to 'kangaroo-bounce' around by launching yourself forwards using both feet. You can also practise collecting samples of rock and soil, and test-drive your surface exploration rover (see pages 34–35)!

LAUNCHING OFF IN LOW GRAVITY

The top section of your lunar landing module can now blast off, using the bottom section as a launch pad. The Apollo astronauts did exactly the same thing when leaving the Moon. Once the engine has been fired, you will head directly upwards to dock with your command module. Because the Moon's gravity is only one-sixth of the Earth's, you can perform these tasks using just tiny bursts from your module's navigational thrusters.

04 TOUR OF THE PLANETS

Each of the planets in the Solar System is a unique world. As far as we know, no being has ever set down on the other seven planets, although robotic probes and spacecraft from Earth have visited all of them. So, these brave new worlds are now yours to explore. You must visit each planet and dig out the data you'll need to survive there.

Kit Checklist:

☐ Command module
☐ Planetary weather satellite
☐ Landing probes
☐ Surface rovers
☐ Gravitational slingshot calculator
☐ Maps of the inner and outer Solar System

Along the way, we can consult the mission log and select the best bits of equipment for each of our missions.

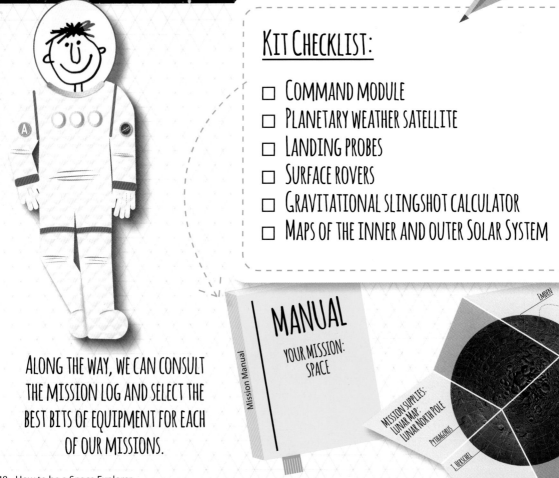

MANUAL
YOUR MISSION: SPACE

Mission Manual

MISSION SUPPLIES:
LUNAR MAP:
LUNAR NORTH POLE

EMDEN
BOLTKOVICH
PYTHAGORAS
J. HERSCHEL

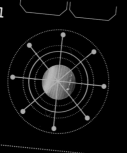

Gravitational
Slingshot
Calculator

Distance: 0.056
Velocity: 1.765
Angle   : 77.67
Radius : 3.528
Axis-tilt:543.7
Density : 167.3

Status Report
9033 65720

Report to Checkpoint

Now you're fully trained, let's apply your lessons to live space. You'll need to pack all the right bits of kit, so that you can make all the right observations about the planets and their systems.

Warning!

You've signed up for the ultimate space adventure. We'll be visiting blazingly hot planets such as Venus, and bone-chilling giants such as Neptune. We'll also go to a very odd place that manages to be unimaginably hot and cold at the same time. **Only the brave should make these journeys.**

As you go along, read about the space missions of the past, so you learn something about the rich history of space exploration. Not many people have done it – you're joining a pretty exclusive club.

Earth's Moon

It may seem odd, starting this tour of ours with our own planet. But Earth is not just our home, it is also the planet against which we judge all others. We're also very lucky to have another world close by – the Moon. We know an awful lot about our nearest neighbour in space, and human missions have landed there six times.

28% LAND

72% WATER

Water Planet

'Earth' is a strange name for our home planet, because it's mostly water. Almost 71 per cent of its surface is covered by the oceans – and another 1 per cent is covered by the water in lakes and rivers. Only 28 per cent of the surface is actually 'earth'. We live on the Blue Planet, or the Water Planet.

LANDING SITE
Field data:
Landing at
3.65, 70.767
3.5km East of Meton

Lunar Orbit

As you see the Moon getting bigger in your spacecraft windows, you are also riding in the slipstream of the Apollo astronauts who orbited the Moon – and landed on its surface – in the 1960s and '70s. By retracing their steps, you can find out what they discovered about the Moon, and how easy it would be for us to set up a base or colony there.

Lunar Landings

A modern washing machine has more computing power than the Mission Control machines that managed to put 12 astronauts on the Moon between 1969 and 1972. Using a more up-to-date version of the landing craft used by those Apollo astronauts, you can now detach from your orbiting spacecraft and travel down to the surface. Check the pre-programmed landing site on your map screen – and use the vehicle's thrusters to control your descent and make a gentle landing.

If you've packed a roving vehicle (see pages 34–35), one of your main tasks is to find out how much water lies in shadowy craters at the Moon's poles. Even if it's frozen, it might be useful for future colonies or bases on the lunar surface. You could also take some readings to find out how sunny it is here. With long periods of sunlight, and no clouds or atmosphere to block it, solar panels could potentially harness a huge amount of energy for a Moon station.

Data Panel: Earth

ADS	:	150M KM
Orbit	:	365 days
Size	:	1xED
Moons	:	1

ROVING AROUND THE SURFACE OF EARTH'S MOON WILL BE GREAT PRACTICE FOR EXPLORING THE MOONS OF OTHER PLANETARY SYSTEMS.

MERCURY

As your spacecraft approaches Mercury, you'll need to set up an orbiting probe to spy on the planet. As the probe descends, look at the images coming back to your craft from its cameras. You'll soon see evidence of the Solar System's wild and violent past.

DEAD PLANET

The cameras on the side of your orbiting probe reveal that the surface of Mercury is scorched and lifeless. There are many craters – these are evidence of the many comets and asteroids that have plummeted into Mercury's landscapes since the planet formed about 4.5 billion years ago.

EXTREME TEMPERATURES

The probe also detects the extreme temperature differences on the surface, which vary by an astounding 600ºC (1100ºF)! Daytime, sunlit temperatures can reach 430ºC (80ºF), but this can plunge to -170ºC (-280ºF) at night. When the planet's orbit brings it closest to the Sun, some of the shadowed areas are cold enough to hold ice!

Data Panel: Mercury

```
ADS     :  58M KM
Orbit   :  88 days
Size    :  0.38xED
Moons   :  0
```

VENUS

Your visit to Venus promises to be a little more explosive. On Earth, at any one time, there are likely to be as many as 20 'active' volcanoes, alive and kicking. But, as we approach Venus, you'll learn we are about to witness the volcanic capital of the Solar System. Release your landing probe – NOW – to find out more.

Data Panel: Venus

ADS	:	108M KM
Orbit	:	225 days
Size	:	0.95xED
Moons	:	0

PARP!

Pressure Planet

As the atmospheric probe descends, its cameras spy a thick blanket of cloud. This is what kept the surface of Venus a mystery for so many years. Probe readings show that the pressure of the atmosphere of Venus is 90 times what it is on Earth. That's enough to crush a submarine. Make sure you download all the data from the landing probe quickly – it will start to melt within one hour!

Probe Report

Touchdown. The cameras sweep the surface and see lava everywhere. It's been brought to the surface – from below the planet's crust – by the eruptions of more than 55,000 separate volcanoes. The lava starts off as hot, molten (semi-fluid) rock, and then slowly cools and hardens to form these incredible landscapes.

Fart Planet

The probe also tells you that the rainfall on Venus is acidic – sulphuric acid, to be precise. But the rain never reaches the ground. The planet also smells of farts. That's the hydrogen sulphide gas, given off by all those volcanoes. All in all, this is not a great destination for a human mission.

MARS

Your flight to Mars has covered 563 million km (350 million miles) in 250 days. Your detachable probe is now cruising at a comfortable speed, high above the Martian surface. Inside your orbiting spacecraft, you now need to set up your science lab.

EARTH'S BROTHER

Why are humans planning to head for Mars? Maybe because it reminds us of home. Like Earth, Mars has weather, it has seasons, and it has polar ice caps. Its days and nights are almost the same length, too.

YOUR MISSION

Your mission is to collect enough data so that the experts back home can plan a manned mission to Mars in the future.

#1

#4

645,379

3.14159 446095505 33936072
2653589 822317253 60249141
7932384 59408128   273
6264338 481117450   7245
3279502 284102701 87006606
8841971 938521105 31558817
6939937 559644622 48815209
510   948954930 20962829
    582 38196   25409171
0974944   536436
5923078 442881097   7892
1640628 566593344 59036001
6208998 612847564 13305305
6280348 823378678 48820466
2534211 316527120 52138414
70679   19091   69519415
    821   45648   11609
4808651 56692346o
3282306 34861045
6470938 432664821

Blue Sunsets

Your robotic rover is now recording videos of a Martian sunset. Around sunset and sunrise, the sky is generally pinkish-red in colour – but nearer to the rising or setting Sun it is blue. This is the exact opposite of what we get on Earth. During the day, the Martian sky is a yellow-brown colour. Your rover's readings suggest that these colours are caused by small amounts of iron compounds – from the rocks and soil – that get blown up into the atmosphere.

Grand Canyon

Meanwhile, the camera on your orbiting probe spies a huge canyon. This is the Mariner Valley. One of the most amazing sights on Earth is the Grand Canyon in Arizona, USA. Our Canyon was carved out by running water, which wore away the rocks over millions of years. Could the Mariner Valley have been created in the same way? Although Mars is only half the size of Earth, the Mariner Valley is three times deeper than the Grand Canyon. It's a whopping 7km (4.5 miles) deep and 4000km (2500 miles) long.

Ice Caps

Some features of the Mariner Valley may have been formed by water, at some point in the Red Planet's early history. This is evidence that Mars, like Earth, may have been wetter and warmer in ancient times. It will need a closer look, when our manned missions eventually touch down on Mars.

Data Panel:
Mars

```
ADS    :  228M KM
Orbit  :  687 days
Size   :  0.53xED
Moons  :  2
```

JUPITER

When planets are as massive and gassy as Jupiter is, they start to have a lot in common with stars. Like the Sun, Jupiter is mostly made up of hydrogen and helium, and it also gives out some heat. In fact, it's 99.9 per cent hydrogen and helium, with just a dash of other elements.

```
Data Panel:
Jupiter

ADS      :  778M KM
Orbit    :  12 years
Size     :  10.93xED
Moons    :  67
```

All this gas means there's no surface on which to land your spacecraft. So you'll have to send out another probe to make your studies.

GIANT WORLD

Many kilometres beneath the brown clouds of hydrogen and helium in Jupiter's atmosphere, your probe is sending back data from a mysterious realm. You begin to see more of what appears to be a planet-wide ocean of liquid hydrogen. The cameras send back images of a dark and dense world, where giant lightning bolts provide only brief moments of light.

GIANT STORM

The weather instruments in your science lab have detected Jupiter's most famous feature – the Great Red Spot. This is a huge storm that once covered 40,000km (24,850 miles) of the surface, but which is now about half this size. So maybe this storm is slowly passing – although we know that it's been raging for at least 400 years! If you focus your cameras on it, you'll see smaller, high-speed whirlpools of wind inside it, which are proof that the storm is still very active.

SATURN

The make-up of Saturn is not unlike that of Jupiter – so, instead of analysing the planet itself, you might decide to steer your spacecraft towards its glorious system of rings. The rings may only be about 1km (0.6 miles) thick, but they reach out to about 80,000km (50,000 miles) above the planet's equator.

But what exactly are the rings made of? You'll need to send out a probe to get a closer look.

Data Panel: Saturn

```
ADS    : 1427M KM
Orbit  : 30 years
Size   : 9xED
Moons  : 62
```

RINGED PLANET

Saturn is also a very gusty world. Your over-worked weather probe has measured winds in the planet's upper atmosphere reaching speeds of 1,800km/h (1,118mph) near to its equator. These gusts are almost five times speedier than the strongest, hurricane-force winds on Earth, which top out at about 396km/h (246mph). These super-fast winds, along with heat rising from the planet's interior, cause the yellow and gold bands you see in Saturn's atmosphere.

BECAUSE SATURN CAN'T BE SAID TO HAVE A SURFACE – SATURN CAN'T BE SAT-ON!

Uranus

If you need to save fuel, why not use a gravitational slingshot to get to the next two planets? This means using the orbit and gravity of a massive planet, such as Saturn, to influence the speed and direction of your spacecraft. Saturn travels at about 10km (6 miles) per second, and a slingshot around it should help you to go twice as fast!

WEEEEEEEEE!!!!!!!!

Mini Systems

The outer planets, from Jupiter to Neptune, are all a little bit like miniature Solar Systems. But, in place of the planets that orbit the Sun, these outer planets are orbited by many moons. Jupiter has at least 67 moons, Saturn has at least 62, Uranus has 27 and Neptune has 14.

Data Panel: Uranus

ADS	:	2871M KM
Orbit	:	84 years
Size	:	3.97×ED
Moons	:	27

Weather Data: Methane Clouds

Take a look at the data and images streaming back from the probe. It's quite a featureless planet, isn't it? If you zoom in a little more, you should be able to make out the wispy, icy clouds of methane in the lower parts of the atmosphere. In fact, it is thanks to the methane in the atmosphere that Uranus has a lovely, cool blue-green colour.

Ice Giant

Uranus is the seventh planet from the Sun. If you release a probe into the upper layers of atmosphere that make up Uranus, you'll see that the planet has a slightly different composition (make-up) to the gas giants, Jupiter and Saturn. Uranus also contains the gases hydrogen and helium, but it also has 'ices' such as water, ammonia, and methane. This is why the two outer giants, Uranus and Neptune, are known as the 'ice giants'.

Neptune

Uranus was the first planet to be discovered using a telescope, in 1781, and it took a tricky bit of maths to locate Neptune! Astronomers were noticing unexpected changes in the orbital path of Uranus. Something pretty massive, with a lot of gravity, seemed to be tugging on it. The experts did their sums and successfully calculated, in 1846, that the object causing the wobbles was none other than Neptune.

Weather Data: Violent Weather

The weather probe is recording wind speeds as high as 2100km/h (1300mph). Inside your on-board science lab, the weather instruments are also telling you that Neptune's outer atmosphere is one of the coldest places in the Solar System, with temperatures at its cloud tops measuring -218°C (-360°F).

Dark Storm

As your weather probe descends into the atmosphere of Neptune, it'll detect a lot more activity than it did inside the atmosphere of Uranus. There are also visible weather patterns here, and from above you will observe that Neptune has a Great Dark Spot. This fabulous feature is driven by the strongest winds of any planet in the Solar System.

Data Panel: Neptune

ADS	:	4498M KM
Orbit	:	165 years
Size	:	3.86xED
Moons	:	14

05 TOURING THE MOONS

Your tour of the planets terminated with the Ice Giants, Uranus and Neptune. Now you've returned to Earth's Lunar Base to fuel-up for your mission to the moons of the outer planets. You are about to visit some of the very coldest places of the Solar System, such as icy Triton, Neptune's major moon, and freezing Ganymede, the largest moon in the entire system.

ROBOTS AT THE READY!

Having toured the planets, you're now a dab hand at programming probes and dropping them down towards the surface of other worlds. Well, investigating moons is not all that different. Many are as large as planets, and some have a thick atmosphere, too, which will block your view from above. So prepare to send more robots into action!

SAVING FUEL

As the Moon's gravity is only one-sixth the strength of Earth's, you can save fuel by using your Moon base as the taking-off point for this next set of missions. From here, a much lower escape velocity is needed (see pages 22–23).

CHILLED OUT

So, what did you find when you roved around our own Moon? Scientists have recently discovered that the dark and sunless craters at the Moon's southern pole are among the coldest places ever recorded. The tall rims of these craters block out the Sun's rays, keeping the crater at a constant temperature of -240°C (-400°F). Compared to that, the freezing places on Earth seem pretty toasty. The coldest temperature ever recorded on Earth was -89°C (-128°F), in Antarctica.

MIND YOUR MOONS!

The dozens of planetary moons in the Solar System vary greatly in size, age and origin. Though these alien worlds will differ, a mission like this will tell you a great deal about the way planets and moons are made and evolve.

EXPLORING THE LEFT-OVERS

You're now on your way to the fascinating planetary moons of the outer Solar System. These interplanetary journeys will leave you with time to surf your computer console, download information and find out as much as you can about the formation of the moons, as well as other 'rocky parts' of the system.

PLANETARY RINGS

Astronomers have two theories as to how Saturn got its amazing rings. Theory one: there was an ancient moon (or several such moons) around Saturn, but its orbit came too close to the giant planet and the force of Saturn's tides ripped it apart. Theory two: the rings are the left-overs of the stuff out of which Saturn was made.

THE 'BIG SPLASH' THEORY

Where did the Moon come from? You might be amazed to find out that it came from the Earth! According to astronomers, an object roughly the size of Mars smashed into the Earth, around 4.5 billion years ago. The force of the impact sent a huge amount of debris into space, some of which was sent into orbit around the Earth until it re-settled together into the Moon.

Mission status:

You are now halfway to the Jupiter system.

Remnant Moons

Moons are remnants from the formation of planets – just as planets are made from the left-overs of star formation. This kind of thing happens whenever there's a disc of material in orbit around a massive central body. Gravity causes most of the stuff to fall inwards to the central body, but some bits remain in orbit, and these become moons. The most massive planets, Jupiter and Saturn, drew the most left-over materials towards them – which is why they have the most moons.

Rings and Bling!

Using data from the Cassini spacecraft, astronomers have found that there's far more ice in the rings than they once thought. The icy bits are closely packed together and bash into each other all the time – so they break apart, bringing new icy faces to the surface. Sunlight reflects off the icy parts, making them bright and easy to see.

Ice Fountains

Saturn's outer rings are constantly being 'refreshed' with shiny new materials. Saturn's icy moon, Enceladus has huge ice fountains that spout out of volcanoes. The moon's gravity is low, so when the volcanoes erupt the icy particles soar up to mind-blowing heights of more than 100km (62 miles). Eventually, the sparkly bits and pieces join one of the outermost rings of Saturn.

Jupiter's Moons

Your spacecraft moves into the Jupiter system. Your approach is dramatic. The Sun, at first hidden by the giant planet, puts on a spectacular sunrise. As it climbs higher, the Sun's brilliant light reflects off Jupiter's main satellites. There are 67 in all, according to your onboard console, but you're focusing on the innermost four, in orbit about the huge expanse of Jupiter.

Callisto

Europa

Great Ganymede

Your spacecraft glides above Ganymede, the largest moon in the Solar System. Wow. On the surface of this massive world, you can see some very old terrain (land). Using your onboard computer to count up the number of craters on Ganymede, you can work out the age of this moon. Just like our Moon, it is about 4.5 *billion* years old.

The Margherita Moon

The surface of Io looks like a giant pizza! It seems to be made of cheese and tomato, but the colours you are seeing – yellow, red, white, black and green – are all different forms of sulphur, one of the main elements churned out by Io's volcanoes. With over 400 active volcanoes – and more than 100 mountains being lifted up by extreme movements in the moon's crust – the surface of this crazy world is constantly changing!

Europa's Ocean

Europa is an ice world. It has a twisted and cracked surface, which looks like those places on Earth where solid ice is floating on water. The big question about Europa is whether, like Callisto, there's an underground ocean beneath this frozen crust. Europa is warmer than Callisto, and more likely to have life forms in its subterranean ocean – if it has one. You might want to think about sending down a probe to drill through the icy crust and investigate what lies beneath it.

Sizing Up Galileo's Moons

Ganymede

Mercury

Callisto

Io

Moon

Europa

Cratered Callisto

Your spacecraft's computer tells you that Callisto has carbon dioxide and oxygen in its thin atmosphere, which sits above the heavily cratered world you see below you now. It's also quite likely that Callisto has an ocean, hidden under its surface.

The four largest moons of Jupiter were discovered by Galileo in 1610, using his home-made telescope. They are known as the Galilean moons in his honour.

Saturn's Moons

As you approach Saturn, the sight of its rings is breath-taking. They stretch into the distance for more than 250,000km (155,343 miles) from your spacecraft – and yet they appear to be razor-thin. The rings are actually less than 1km (0.6 miles) in thickness, and in some places they are as thin as 10m (33ft).

TITAN

SATURN'S LARGEST MOON

Titan: Factoids

#1

It's larger than Mercury, and almost 50 per cent bigger than our own Moon.

#2

It's the second -largest moon in the Solar System, after Ganymede.

#3

But more importantly, Titan is the only moon we've found – so far – that has a thick, dense atmosphere.

Shepherd Moons

The 'shepherd' moons of Saturn are very small moons that orbit near the outer edges of the rings, or within gaps in the rings. Their gravity helps to hold the shape of the beautiful ring structure together. Saturn has 62 official moons, although it also holds countless other 'moonlets' in its powerful gravity-grip.

The Cassini-Huygens Mission

In 2005, the unmanned Cassini spacecraft flew to Saturn to investigate the planet. It carried the Huygens probe, named after Christiaan Huygens – the Dutch scientist who discovered Titan. The probe detached itself from Cassini and plummeted into Titan's atmosphere. A great parachute was deployed. Huygens then sank slowly down through the organic haze, taking readings as it went, and finally set upon the surface of this world. It found that, although Titan is very cold, it is rich in the organic ingredients needed to get life going, both on its surface and in its seas.

Probe Readings

Your own landing probe has begun to send back its data and images… Like the early Earth, Titan is an organic world, rich in nitrogen. The atmosphere is full of wind, clouds and black rain. You can make out what appear to be sand dunes, and maybe a river. The Cassini–Huygens mission found murky seas, or possibly lakes, made of liquid methane and ethane. You check the probe's cameras once more, and spy what looks like a wave on the surface of the sea.

Neptune's Moons

The final destination of your moons tour is the neighbourhood of Neptune, a distant system of chilly worlds. You now sit, all on your own, with only the voices from Mission Control for company – but you are now so far from Earth that those messages from home are taking 246 minutes to reach you. So, while you wait, enjoy a view that no other human has witnessed.

Orbiting Oddly

Triton is Neptune's biggest moon by far, and the seventh-largest moon in the Solar System. It takes almost six Earth days for Triton to do a single orbit of Neptune – and, weirdly, it orbits in the opposite direction to which its planet spins. This suggests that Triton is not native to Neptune. Instead it is a 'captured' moon, probably pulled in from the outer reaches of the Solar System by Neptune's gravity.

KEY

- - - - -
Triton spinning on its axis

- - - - -
Triton orbits around Neptune in the opposite direction

Neptune has only been explored once before, when the unmanned Voyager 2 mission visited it in 1989. The serene blue of this huge, ringed planet sits below you as your spacecraft makes its way to the most fascinating of Neptune's 14 known moons – Triton.

Triton is an active world. When the Voyager 2 mission visited, it saw geyser-like eruptions spewing up – 8km (5 miles) into the atmosphere. The plumes of material jetting out from the eruptions are, according to your own probe, made of invisible nitrogen gas and dust from beneath the surface of Triton. This explains why the surface looks so fresh and new. Volcanic material from inside Triton is being deposited in vast amounts, all over its plains and terrains.

Probe Readings

You've sent a probe down to Triton, and it has already sensed its nitrogen-rich atmosphere, similar to Titan's (see pages 66–67). But as the atmosphere is much thinner here, you can see the surface of the moon very clearly. It's an alien world of ices – there's nitrogen ice, methane ice, and (under those ices) probably water ice and rock. You also see impact basins, craters, long valleys and vast plains covered with freshly fallen nitrogen snow.

06 CHASING SPACE ROCKS

The action does not stop at Neptune. There are many other worlds beyond the eight planets – but, since they are much smaller, you can refer to them as 'worldlets'. For all you know, a huge Planet X could be lurking in the darkness beyond Neptune. But for now, you must focus your gaze on the smaller space rocks of the Solar System.

BEYOND NEPTUNE

Until the 20th century, the realms of space beyond Neptune were a complete mystery to scientists and astronomers.

You are about to explore a region of space that – until recently – only existed in the theories and minds of astronomers. Through the power of science and exploration, the theory has been turned into fact, and your mission is to find more evidence for what's out there. **Be warned – it may be a little like looking for a black cat in a dark cellar!**

KEEP YOUR EYES PEELED!

Comets and asteroids travel at high speeds, through a Solar System that can get quite busy and congested. Just a glancing collision with one of those high-velocity space rocks could end your mission, for good!

Kit Checklist:

- ☐ COMMAND MODULE
- ☐ DATABASE OF KNOWN COMETS AND ASTEROIDS
- ☐ MAP OF THE OUTER SOLAR SYSTEM
- ☐ COMET ORBIT CALCULATOR
- ☐ DIRECTIONS TO THE OORT CLOUD
- ☐ LANDING PROBES

KEEP AN EYE ON HISTORY!

Remember, much can be learnt not only from your own experience so far, but also from the space exploration missions of the past. Download the history module now!

COMET/ASTEROID DATABASE

(29075) 1950 DA
Churyumov-
Gerasimenko
Halley's Comet
9p/Tempel
107 Camilla

Welcome aboard your deep-space mission. Hold on tight!

MISSION MANIFESTO

BITS AND BOBS

It's a long journey, and you've been looking out through the windows of your spacecraft. At first, you see just a trickle of small worlds. Soon, though, your craft approaches a vast array of these worldlets. The computer says they extend from the orbit of Pluto halfway to the nearest star.

Asteroid Belt

Field data:
Unspecified distance
Pluto---Proxima Centauri
Billions of unidentified
objects----space debris

Near-Earth Objects

There may be several million asteroids in the Belt, although most of them are thousands of kilometres apart. Main-belt asteroids usually stay at home – but sometimes they like to wander. There are hundreds of asteroids whose path takes them near to Earth. Together with comets and other debris, these are known as Near-Earth Objects, or NEOs. In the past, when NEOs have smashed into the Earth, life has been dramatically affected (see pages 78–79).

Failed Planets

These rocky leftovers are asteroids, comets and (sometimes) small moons. They are all the same types of building blocks that the planets were made out of, early in the history of the Solar System. The word asteroid means 'star-like', but asteroids are far from it. Some are rocky, others are metallic – and some are rich in the organic materials from which life forms are composed.

THE ASTERIOD BELT

With the aid of your computer, you can work out that none of these objects is more than 1000km (620 miles) across. The main region of asteroids in the Solar System actually lies much closer to the Sun – in between Mars and Jupiter. This area of orbiting material is known as the Asteroid Belt.

BUILDING THE BELT

Astronomers used to think the Asteroid Belt was the remains of a demolished world – but many now prefer a different theory. Most of the asteroid-like worldlets went into building the planets, but the presence of mighty Jupiter – with its huge gravitational tug – prevented some of the building blocks from becoming a new world. So, the Belt seems to be the remains of a world destined never to be.

Shooting Stars

1. Meteoroid

In space, a small rocky or metallic body is known as a meteoroid. They're much smaller than asteroids, ranging in size from small grains to 1m (3ft) wide. Most are fragments from asteroids and comets, and a few fall down to the Earth.

2. Meteor

The trail of their entry through the Earth's atmosphere is known as a meteor, or 'shooting star'.

3. Meteorite

Once the meteoroids have hit the ground, they're known as meteorites. But don't worry – accidents caused by falling meteorites are rare.

EYES TO THE SKIES

Ann Hodges – of Alabama, USA – had a lucky escape in 1954 when a 4kg (9lb) meteorite crashed through the roof of her house, bounced off her radio and then hit her! Luckily, she was only bruised.

Your spacecraft has now entered the realms of the Oort Comet Cloud. It's impossible to guess the shape of the Cloud from the view through your windows. But the computer shows that the Cloud is a huge ball-shape, made up of a trillion objects – that's a million million! The comets are mostly made of ices, such as water, ammonia and methane.

GAS TAIL

DUST TAIL

A

COMET DANCE

The outer edge of the Sun's Oort Cloud may stretch halfway to the nearest star. Not every other star has an Oort Cloud, but many probably do. As the Sun passes nearby stars, its Oort Cloud will encounter other comet clouds. The average distance between comets in these clouds is about the distance from Earth to Mars. So the passing clouds won't collide – instead, their objects will 'dance past' each other.

COMET TAILS

Now, watch your display screen to see the journey of a comet. It begins as a frozen and inactive rock, out here in the Oort Cloud. Then, as it wings its way toward the Sun, the Sun's radiation causes materials on the comet to stream out into space. This is known as a 'tail', and comets normally have two. One tail will be made up of gassy materials, while the other is made of dusty stuff.

DIRTY SNOWBALLS

Comets are space rocks that make a regular orbit around the Sun. If you check your computer display, you'll see that they are a bit like 'dirty snowballs' – a mixture of rock and ice. Comet nuclei (centres) vary quite a bit in size, too – from about 0.75km (0.5 miles) to as much as 20km (12 miles) in diameter. On average, they are more like 10km (6 miles) wide.

OORT CLOUD: ORIGIN

The puzzle is… how did all those comets get out into the Cloud in the first place? Some scientists say the comets were ejected out of the Solar System by the gravity fields of the giant planets, such as Jupiter. Others think that a lot of the Oort Cloud objects were made when the Sun and nearby stars formed and then drifted apart.

Oort Cloud: The Evidence

The planets of the Solar System have roughly oval-shaped, or elliptical, orbits. The orbits of comets are cigar-shaped, or parabolic. The planets all orbit the Sun in the same flat plane, but comets can come winging in from any direction. That's why astronomers think the Oort Cloud exists. If the comets can wing in from anywhere, then they must completely surround the Solar System.

Close Encounters

Comets and asteroids have been around since the start of the Solar System, so it's a good idea to get to know them better. You might want to steer your spacecraft closer – or even take a ride on one! The European Space Agency (ESA) have had the very same plan for their Rosetta spacecraft.

Speeding through Space

So, how fast do comets go when they get close to the Sun? Let's look at a famous example – Halley's comet. It travels at 1km (0.6 miles) per second when it's way out from the Sun. But as it approaches the Sun its speed rises to an incredible 50km (30 miles) a second.

Journey Highlights

In July 2005, after its launch in March 2004, Rosetta witnessed another comet encounter. This was the collision of the NASA space probe Deep Impact with the comet 9P/Tempel. The Deep Impact mission deliberately smashed into the comet so that it could sample the material inside it. NASA found that Tempel was dustier and less icy than expected. Rosetta recorded the event and downlinked the science data to Earth.

MISSION BRIEFING: ROSETTA

Since its launch, in March 2004, the ESA's Rosetta spacecraft has completed a flyby of the Earth and Mars, taking a close look at asteroids 2867 Ŝteins and 21 Lutetia as it did so. Then it went into deep-space hibernation for more than two years. In 2014, the spacecraft 'woke up' and got ready to chase a comet called Churyumov–Gerasimenko around the Sun!

Rosetta Probe

Rosetta: The Spacecraft

The Rosetta spacecraft has two main parts. The first part is the Rosetta probe itself, which has 12 main instruments. The second is its robotic lander, Philae, which has a further 9 instruments. The main probe instruments include cameras, devices to measure the composition of the comet, and other gadgets to find out what gas and dust is in the comet's tail.

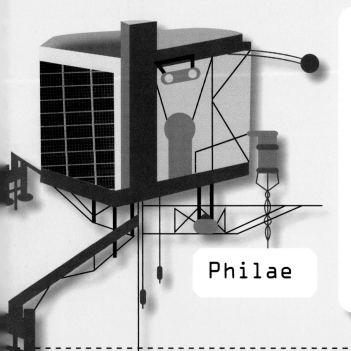

Philae

Philae's Mission

To land on comet Churyumov–Gerasimenko, the robotic lander, Philae, must first gain enough speed to catch up with it. The ESA decided to catch the comet when it's closest to the Sun, which is when it's moving at its fastest. Philae will deploy harpoons to anchor itself to the surface, then it will hold on tight. The lander's legs are designed to soften the impact to stop Philae from bouncing off! The lander will then study the comet's surface for a week – but a longer mission, lasting for months, is also possible.

BIG WIPE-OUTS

What's the biggest piece of evidence you've gathered so far? It could be the fact that most rocky bodies in the Solar System – particularly the moons – are simply covered with craters. On this trip, you've seen hundreds and hundreds of them – either through your spacecraft window or in the images sent back by your robotic rovers and probes.

VIOLENT NEIGHBOURHOOD

You've also witnessed the culprits of all that crater damage. The space in between the planets is littered with a huge collection of rogue worldlets – such as comets and asteroids – that are free to roam and do a lot of damage, should anything get in their way. You can't help but come to the conclusion that Earth lives in a pretty violent neighbourhood!

COLLISIONS WITH EARTH

For every crater on the Moon, there should be hundreds on the Earth – but the evidence is harder to find. Earth is a live and volcanic planet, with plates of crust that move across its surface. This means the craters get covered up as Earth 'renews' its rocky upper layers. However, if you dig beneath the surface, some very large craters are there to be found.

BOMBARDED WORLDS

As you journey back towards your Moon Base, for refuelling, you see images of the lunar surface flash up on your computer's display screen. The Moon is so ravaged by holes and craters that there must have been a time – billions of years ago – when the Solar System was in a wild turmoil! The Moon's many scars are proof that the system's rocky leftovers continued to bombard the planets and moons long after they were formed.

PHEW!

HIDDEN CRATERS

The discovery of huge craters in the Earth's crust proves that Earth was heavily bombarded in its early days – just as often as the Moon was. In fact, by studying these impact craters geologists have been able to divide the history of the Earth into different time periods. For example, the impact that did away with the dinosaurs, about 65 million years ago, marked the end of the Cretaceous period and the beginning of the Paleogene, which lasted until roughly 23 million years ago.

WILL HUMANS BECOME DINOSAURS?

Astronomers keep a keen eye on the sky – for a very good reason. There are hundreds of known asteroids in near-Earth orbits and millions of comets lurking out in deeper space – AND we have enough evidence from history to show that their impacts can have a shocking effect on life on our planet. One such near-Earth object is an asteroid known as (29075) 1950 DA. It was first thought to be on a possible collision course with Earth in the year 2880, but now it seems it will be a 'near-miss'.

07 VOLCANIC ADVENTURES

Volcanoes are not found only on Earth. They are found on any moon or planet with a solid crust and hot, molten rock inside. We can even see evidence of mountains that are actually ancient volcanoes, no longer active. So it's time for you to become a volcano detective. Studying volcanoes on other worlds also improves our understanding of those on Earth, helping us to predict violent eruptions and save lives.

Stay On Your Spacecraft!

Unless otherwise advised by Mission Control, it's best you **stay inside your spacecraft** on this trip, at least when you're anywhere near volcanoes. Not only are they explosively dangerous, but they also give off the most noxious and smelly gases.

It's Time

ime for you to look deep into the past and become a volcano detective!

Greek philosopher Empedocles is best known for saying that all stuff is made of the four elements; earth, air, fire and water. But there's also a famous legend about the way in which he ended his life. The story goes that Empedocles died by throwing himself into Mount Etna, one of Earth's most famous volcanoes. Empedocles wanted onlookers to believe that he had turned into an immortal god. But the volcano ruined his plan by vomiting back one of his sandals. Empedocles was unlikely to be a god if he couldn't even remember to take his shoes along to the afterlife!

THE 1815 ERUPTION OF MOUNT TAMBORA — IN INDONESIA, ON PLANET EARTH — IS THE LARGEST EVER RECORDED BY HUMANS. IT EXPLODED SO LOUDLY THAT IT WAS HEARD MORE THAN 2000KM (1200 MILES) AWAY.

Volcano Hunting

As you orbit the Earth, you sometimes see mountains that seem to have had their tops chopped off. These mountains have wide holes, or craters, at their peaks. Some craters look small from where you are, while others are almost as broad as the mountain itself. You fly over craters filled with water, and others containing the most amazing molten material.

Mount Pelée

When Mount Pelée erupted, in 1902, the city of Saint-Pierre – on the Caribbean island of Martinique – was devastated. A hot, glowing volcanic cloud swept down its slopes and killed approximately 35,000 people.

FIERY CAULDRONS

Once the hot, molten magma reaches the surface, around the crater, it becomes lava – the thick, sticky, liquefied rock that pours down the sides of the volcano. Its temperature is 700–1200°C (1292–2192°F). Some volcanoes also throw jets of magma up to 200m (660ft) into the atmosphere.

THE EARTH EXPLODES

Volcanoes are all different in shape, size and power – and they can erupt in many different ways. Before an eruption, there are normally tremors in the earth. The eruption itself then blasts the top part of the mountain into the sky, causing torrents of rock and ash to rain down over a wide area. This is usually the most destructive part of an eruption.

MOLTEN MAGMA

Volcanoes are basically weak spots on a planet or moon where hot, molten (semi-liquid) rock – called magma – can get out. The magma wells up and fills the chamber beneath the volcanic vent, which is blocked off by hardened rock from previous eruptions of molten material. This is where the magma mingles with gas and water to produce an explosive mixture. Pressure then builds up until the hardened material above the vent is pulverised, often resulting in a huge explosion.

MAGMA CHAMBER

CRUST

UPPER MANTLE

LOWER MANTLE

CORE

FINDING EARTH'S HOT SPOTS

There may be as many as 1500 active volcanoes on Earth. Some, beneath the seas, are yet to be discovered. Beneath them are oceans of magma, which is what the Earth's solid crust – its outermost, rocky shell – is floating on. The crust is broken up into 'tectonic plates'. There are seven or eight major plates and many minor ones. Volcanoes are most likely to be found where these plates meet. But volcanoes can also be found at so-called 'hot spots' – for example Hawaii – where magma is able to well up from deep in the Earth.

Volcanic Worlds

Now it's time to download some more information from your onboard computer. You need to recognise all the different features of terrestrial (Earth-based) volcanoes, so that you'll be able to spot the same features on other rocky planets and moons in the Solar System. **What is it that they all have in common?**

Hot Insides

Eruptions of lava on Earth tell us that the Earth's inside parts are very hot. The Earth's crust is about 6–40km (4–25 miles) thick, and below this layer lies the mantle. The upper parts of the mantle, where it meets the crust, can be as hot as 500–900°C (932–1652°F). Scorching! The interior is hot and molten for two main reasons. Firstly, there are radioactive elements down there, such as uranium, which give off heat as they decay. Secondly, the Earth is still hot from its fiery formation, around 4.5 billion years ago!

Inside Rocky Worlds

When many small worldlets clump together to make a rocky planet, the denser, more metallic stuff sinks to the centre, while the less dense materials rise to the surface. That's why Earth has a dense iron core. This is also one of the reasons why the Earth is hotter towards the centre. Some of this internal heat needs to be let out, into the atmosphere, so that the planet can cool down and stop overheating. This is why a lot of rocky planets and moons have volcanoes.

Cooling Down

So, how do volcanoes become safe-looking mountains? Your computer can answer this for you now. Tall volcanoes have been built up by layer upon layer of molten material, which has spewed out onto the surface while the volcano was active. Once a volcano becomes inactive, or dormant, all of that material can cool down and solidify. Then the volcano resembles a peaceful mountain.

PLAN YOUR ROUTE

Programme your navigation system to head for Mars, the next stop on your volcanic adventure. Your spacecraft will use the flyby gravity of Mars to propel you to the outer Solar System, where you will visit Io, one of Jupiter's big moons. Then you can use Jupiter's immense gravity to fling you back to Venus, the volcanic capital of the Solar System.

UNDERWATER VENTS

Robotic probes and crewed submarines have been down to visit the ocean vents, which are usually about 2000–3000m (6600–9800ft) below the surface of the sea. Powered by volcanic activity, they release plumes of super-heated, mineral-rich water. The sea around the vent may be only 2°C (36°F), but the water spewing from the vents ranges from 60°C (140°F) to 464°C (867°F)! Deep-sea explorers have discovered entire ecosystems down there (see pages 108–109).

VOLCANIC VENTS

Vents are important, too, and something to look out for on your volcano tour. A vent is a 'fissure' – a long, narrow opening in a planet's surface where magma escapes and becomes lava. Some vents are flat-looking cracks, and many vents are on the ocean floor. All the major oceans also have mid-ocean ridges. These are chains of underwater mountains where new lava bubbles up, creating brand-new plains of crust on the ocean floor.

Martian Megavolcanoes

Your spacecraft has arrived in orbit around Mars. By now, this planet is a familiar destination for you – but what you see through the window comes as a bit of a surprise. The red planet you expected to see is completely covered by a global dust storm. The only features you can make out are four circular spots, rising out of the pinkish murk. As you look closer you see that these Martian mountain-tops have holes in them… They could be volcanoes!

Martian Volcanoes

Later, after your spacecraft has circled the planet a few times, the storm begins to clear. As you make another pass, you can see that those four features are indeed huge volcanic mountains. They are poking through the dust clouds, each one capped with a vast caldera, or crater, at the summit.

Colossal Caldera

The caldera on Olympus Mons is a colossal 85km (53 miles) wide. The volcano, overall, is extremely broad at its base, stretching across 624km (374 miles). So, Olympus Mons covers an area of the Martian surface that is roughly the size of the state of Arizona in the USA!

Olympus Mons

When the dust has completely settled, the full might of the volcanoes is stunning. The largest of them is called Olympus Mons, or Mount Olympus. In Greek mythology, Mount Olympus is the lofty home of the gods. This giant mammoth volcano is more than 25km (16 miles) high. That's immense! It dwarfs not just the largest volcanoes on Earth, but also the largest mountain, Everest, which stands at only 8.8km (5.5 miles) above the plains of Tibet, in Asia.

PROBE REPORT

Your robotic rover is still on the Martian surface (see pages 54–55) and has been trundling across to Olympus Mons to take a closer look for you. As it angles its cameras upwards, you can see a huge escarpment, or cliff, surrounding the outer edge of the volcano. It rises to 10km (6 miles) above the surrounding plains. Olympus Mons is so huge and heavy that its immense weight causes the Martian crust to sink slightly underneath it. Through the rover's cameras, you can see a wide depression, or dip, around the base of the volcano – a tell-tale sign of its overwhelming weight!

OLYMPUS MONS

MOUNT EVEREST

SUPER SHIELD

While downloading more information from the onboard computer, you discover that Olympus Mons is categorised as a 'shield' volcano. These exist on Earth, too. Instead of violently spewing out lava, shield volcanoes are created as lava flows down their flanks quite slowly. Over a huge amount of time, the volcanoes build up in shape – but they have a low, squat appearance, rather than the more 'pointed' look of other terrestrial volcanoes.

OLYMPUS MONS IS SO HUGE THAT AN ASTRONAUT STANDING ON MARS WOULD BE UNABLE TO SEE THE ENTIRE VOLCANO, EVEN FROM A DISTANCE. THE CURVATURE OF MARS WOULD HIDE MUCH OF IT.

INCREDIBLE IO

Your tour of the Solar System's volcanic sites has been wonderful so far, and now it's time to venture into deeper space again. You have just arrived in the Jupiter system, and you're watching in astonishment as a volcanic fountain on Io spews material into space. Around 250km (155 miles) into space, to be precise. That's higher above Io than some astronauts have ventured above the Earth.

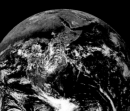

ACTIVE PLUMES

After checking your data screens, you discover that this explosive activity is coming from a volcano called Pele – named after the Hawaiian volcano goddess. But it's not the only active volcano you can see through your windows. In total there are 10 active plumes pouring gas and fine particles into the Ionian sky.

Probe Mission

You saw evidence of the colours of Io's surface on your last visit to the Jupiter system (see pages 64–65). Those colours are mainly down to the presence of sulphur, one of the main ingredients spewed out by Io's volcanoes. You send a probe down to the surface to take some temperature readings. Earth's insides are hot because of radioactivity and the heat from its formation. But Io is hot due to the huge gravitational pull of Jupiter.

Voyager's Visits

Count yourself lucky! You're seeing two more active plumes than the unmanned Voyager 1 spacecraft saw when it first visited Io in March 1979. By the time Voyager 2 had arrived at Io, four months later, Pele had turned itself off, but all the other plumes were still active. Io is clearly a very volcanic moon.

GANYMEDE

EUROPA

IO

OUCH!

PROBE REPORT

The volcano-making heat energy on Io is caused by tides. On Earth, the tides of the oceans are created by the gravitational pulling effect of the Sun and Moon. On Io, there is no water – but the gravity of planet Jupiter and other moons (such as Europa and Ganymede) is tugging at the rocky surface of Io. This squeezes the moon in and out, in the same way as Earth's seas are squeezed and re-shaped into tides. The constant re-shaping of Io creates the interior heat that the volcanoes need to release – and makes parts of the surface rise and fall by anything up to 100m (330ft).

YOUR SPACECRAFT NOW TAKES A SLINGSHOT AROUND JUPITER AND HEADS BACK TOWARDS THE VOLCANIC CAPITAL OF THE INNER SOLAR SYSTEM...

JUPITER

VOLCANIC CAPITAL

Back in orbit around Venus, you see a thick blanket of cloud that blocks out the entire surface of the planet. Fortunately, many missions have been here before and have mapped out what lies below the clouds. In fact, more is known about the surface of Venus than the oceans of Earth!

THE MAGELLAN MISSION

In 1990–93 the NASA unmanned Magellan spacecraft sent back heaps of data on the landforms of Venus. Much of the planet's geology is unlike anything you've seen on Earth, so be sure to keep your wits about you!

Hot, hot, hot...

Your probe from the previous trip to Venus (see pages 52–53) confirms that the surface temperature is in the region of 470ºC (878ºF). That means the Venusian rocks are close to their melting points, which makes them far more soft and flowing than rocks on Earth. Venus is covered in volcanic plains and highland plateaus.

Through the probe's cameras, you can see volcanic cones, shield volcanoes and calderas. In many places, lava has erupted in huge floods.

Spiders

Some of the data sent back by the Magellan mission had Earth geologists puzzled. Some of the curious features on the plains of Venus were more than 200km (124miles) in size. The geologists nicknamed them 'arachnoids' – or 'spiderlike things' – as one of the features had a centre surrounded by long, spindly surface cracks that looked like legs. It's possible that they are volcanic vents.

Esmeralda

Pancakes

Your probe is also sending back pictures of the flat 'pancake domes', which have also confused our scientists. There's nothing like them on Earth. Some think the pancakes may be formed when magma bubbles up from beneath the planet's surface. Instead of breaking through a vent, the magma makes a shallow dome that then collapses again, leaving a pancake-shaped dome behind. It's a rich menu of mysteries!

Gladys and Esmeralda are 'arachnauts' – spiders that lived on the ISS! Scientists watch them via cameras to see if they display any cosmic behaviour.

Gladys

Total Wipe-out

The Magellan spacecraft revealed that the surface of Venus is very young. Some of its volcanoes may still be active, which means parts of the surface get 'refreshed' with new lava flows from time to time. Your probe has done the maths – Venus is at least 4500 million years old, and everything older than 500 million years on its surface has been wiped away. This means Venus was once SO volcanic that it flooded its craters, mountains and other geological features with flow after flow of lava.

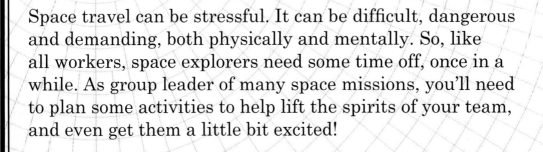

08 EXTREME SPACE

Space travel can be stressful. It can be difficult, dangerous and demanding, both physically and mentally. So, like all workers, space explorers need some time off, once in a while. As group leader of many space missions, you'll need to plan some activities to help lift the spirits of your team, and even get them a little bit excited!

Luxury Europan *Cruises*

Kit Checklist:

☐ Interplanetary holiday brochures
☐ Deep-water diving suit
☐ Mountain-climbing ropes
☐ Safety helmet (with torch)
☐ Knee pads and elbow pads
☐ Bungee rope and harness

EXTREME SPACE
ADMITS ONE

WHO GETS TO GO..?

To begin with, space vacations will be an exotic treat for only the most wealthy people on our planet. At the moment, the cost of travelling into space runs into millions of pounds. So, as a space trainee, you should count yourself lucky that you're getting these fun leisure experiences for free!

THE SOLAR SYSTEM IS NOW OPEN FOR VISITORS!

Explore once-inaccessible frontiers and experience a wealth of intriguing adventures. From low-gravity super-jumps on Miranda to diving in the mysterious seas of Europa, you'll discover many activities that can be enjoyed outside Earth.

TO:
DARING EARTHLINGS
OF PLANET EARTH

SPACE TOURISM

An internet survey asked about people's feelings about holidaying in space. Out of those who replied, 70 per cent wished to holiday for one or two weeks in space, 88 per cent wanted to try a spacewalk, and 21 per cent preferred to chill out in a space hotel or space station.

SPACEWALK
88%

HOLIDAY
70%

CHILL
21%

Extreme Earth

The natural conditions on planet Earth have often encouraged the bold explorer to try out a more challenging sort of sport. These activities make exciting use of our planet's more extreme features, such as its deep oceans, high altitudes, thick atmosphere, and its fairly decent amount of gravity.

Bungee Jumping

This activity involves taking a huge jump from a tall structure while attached to a harness and a long, elastic cord. The jumpers experience the extreme thrill of free-fall during the jump, and then the springy bounce – or rebound – when recoiling after the rope has reached its maximum stretch point.

You could bungee elsewhere in the solar system. How about off the cliffs on Miranda?

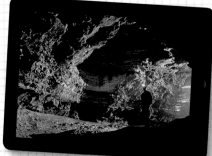

The Mammoth Cave in Kentucky, USA, is more than 650km (405 miles) long!

DIVING BACK TO EARTH

The world's most famous skydiver is an Austrian daredevil called Felix Baumgartner. Felix set the world record for skydiving an incredible 39km (24 miles) in 2012, when he reached a speed of around 1358km/h (844mph). He become the first person to break the sound barrier (without using a vehicle) on his descent.

SPELUNKING

Spelunking, or caving, is the sport of exploring wild cave systems. It can be very dark and wet in the caves, so this activity can be dangerous. It requires a lot of safety kit, including hard hats, artificial torches, ropes, harnesses, ladders and protective clothing.

SKYDIVING

This is where people jump out of an aircraft and return to Earth – the fast way! The first part of the descent is by free-fall. The air resistance provided by our thick atmosphere slows the diver down to a constant speed. A parachute is then deployed and used to create much more air resistance. This slows down the diver for the final stage of the descent – and a safe landing.

DEEP-WATER DIVING

Scuba-diving on Earth is usually done in shallow waters, down to a depth of about 50m (165ft). Even atmospheric 'hard suits' are unable to cope with the pressures of waters beyond about 610m (2000ft) – so, to go deeper, submarines and submersibles are used. The deepest part of the world's ocean is the Mariana Trench, which is more than 10km (6.8 miles) deep.

ONLY TWO SUBMARINE VEHICLES IN HISTORY HAVE EVER REACHED THE DEEPEST KNOWN POINT OF THE MARIANA TRENCH.

MARS: INSIDE AND OUT

Earthlings hope to colonise Mars by the end of the century. Once the colonists have arrived there, they'll need stuff to do as they wait for the fuel to be generated for the return to Earth. Some Earth-based pastimes can be done on Mars, too, with the safety advantage of 38 per cent (of Earth's) gravity.

A slope of five per cent has a ratio of '1:20'. This means you go 20 paces horizontally for every pace downhill. A slope like that doesn't even need a handrail!

5%

MONS MADNESS

The Solar System's largest volcano, Olympus Mons, could be a focus for fun. As the mountain is so huge it would tower above the surrounding Martian plains, but your views from its slopes would depend on how much dust was circulating in the atmosphere. The slopes have a gradient of five per cent, on average, which means they are actually very gentle.

THE MONS CALDERA

The slope around the volcano's caldera (see pages 86–87) is too rough for skateboarding, so let's try abseiling! There's nowhere better to abseil than into the very heart of the volcano. This caldera is an interesting one: it has six collapsed summits, stacked on top of one another, creating a depression at the summit that is 85km (53 miles) wide.

SAFETY SWARM

If you fancy spelunking in the Martian caves, you might want to send out a robotic surveillance team first. Thousands of 10cm-wide (4in-wide), spherical robots could act as a swarm to locate and explore the caves - to find out if they are safe for human exploration. The robots hop around on a powered leg, and have cameras and sensors to explore the caverns in safety. After all, these caves could be pitch black, with almost vertical walls!

CHILL OUT CAVES NOW OPEN!

Abseiling the Abyss

You can abseil with just a long piece of rope. But beware: the rope must be at least twice as long as the cliff you want to go down, and the depth of this caldera is about 3km (1.85 miles). Hopefully, you can find a ledge somewhere. You're abseiling on the Red Planet!

Martian Caverns

A series of caves are cut into the Martian surface, high up on the sides of the planet's other massive volcanoes. There are at least seven caves that would be cool to explore. They also offer protection from radiation, so they're very good places to 'chill out'.

A LOWER GRAVITY ON MARS MEANS THAT IF YOU FALL OVER, IT MIGHT NOT BE SO HARD A FALL!

MISSION BRIEFING: ALIEN OCEAN CHALLENGE

Your previous missions to Europa have unearthed enough data to make the exploration of its alien seas a top attraction. But how should you explore Europa's deep ocean further? And can you learn anything from the extreme science of exploring Earth's deepest and most 'alien' seas?

STUDY THE MISSIONS

NASA's Jupiter Icy Moons Orbiter – or JIMO – was being designed to explore Europa while parked in orbit. A cryobot 'melt-probe' was going to be used to pierce the icy crust. Then, a hydrobot underwater probe would gather data and send it back to Earth. These plans were sadly abandoned in 2005, but could such a mission still go ahead one day…?

CONTAMINATION ALERT!

IF ORGANISMS ARE FOUND IN EUROPA'S SEAS, WE NEED TO BE SURE THEY WON'T CATCH A RIDE BACK TO EARTH!

LANDING MISSIONS

Take a look at NASA's plans for a Europa Lander, first drawn up in 2005. The NASA scientists want to explore the moon's potential for life by testing the ocean water – both within and below Europa's icy shell (see pages 64–65). An even bolder plan would be to delve down deep and get under that icy crust.

DEEPSEA CHALLENGER

Deepsea Challenger is a deep-diving submersible, designed to reach the bottom of Challenger Deep, the deepest part of the Mariana Trench – up to 10,916m (35,814ft) below the surface of the Pacific Ocean. The sub is 7.3m (24ft) long and can hold only one passenger. Movie director James Cameron piloted the sub to reach Challenger Deep in 2012.

ALIENS OF THE DEEP

'Aliens of the Deep' is a documentary in which James Cameron teams up with scientists – from both Russia and NASA – to explore 10 hydrothermal vents in the Atlantic and Pacific oceans. By revealing the creatures that exist and thrive around such vents, the film shows us what life forms on Europa might look like.

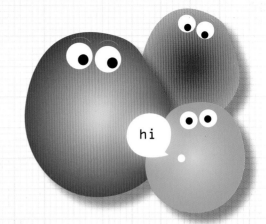

THE EUROPA CHALLENGE

Your own mission could be a combination of the three other mission briefs shown here. You'd need a lander as your base station on Europa. You'd need a giant cryobot to melt the moon's icy crust. And you'd need a submersible - like the Deepsea Challenger - to fully investigate the volcanic vents, way down in the Europan deep.

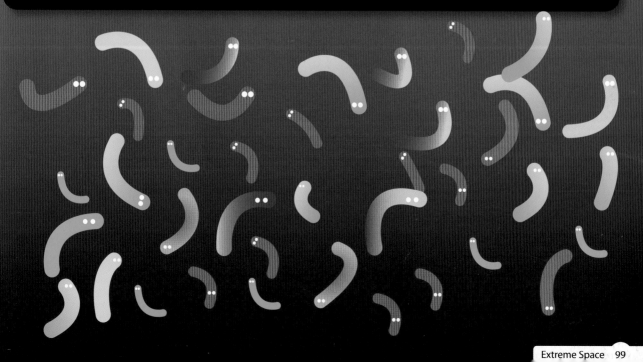

JUMPING THE JIGSAW MOON

Miranda, the smallest and innermost of Uranus's five major moons, is often called the 'jigsaw moon'. Its strange surface looks like a collection of jumbled-up puzzle pieces. But Miranda's crazy, mixed-up surface actually makes it the best place in the Solar System to do a bungee jump.

CLIFFHANGER

Miranda is a geological wonder world, a patchwork moon of huge canyons, racetrack-like ridges and enormous cliffs. These unusual surface features are the result of tidal heating (see page 89), from a time when its orbit was more irregular. But it's the cliffs, standing as high as 20km (12.4 miles), that will interest the bungee jumper.

Verona Rupes is the tallest cliff on Miranda, at 20km (12.4 miles) high. The tallest one on Earth is Canada's Mount Thor, which is a 1.25km (0.78-mile) drop.

FREE-FALLING

On Earth, when intrepid skydivers – such as Felix Baumgartner (see pages 94–95) – free-fall from an aircraft, their motion through the air is limited. The force of gravity causes them to be attracted towards the centre of the Earth – but they are also experiencing the resistance created by particles in the air. This resistance slows their speed.

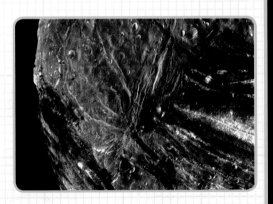

MIRANDA'S HIGHEST CLIFFS

What would it be like to jump off Verona Rupes? There is no atmosphere on Miranda, so there would be no air resistance. The gravity there is also incredibly weak. The 20km (12.8-mile) jump would therefore take about 12 minutes. In comparison, Felix Baumgartner's jump (see page 95) – from 39km (24 miles) above the Earth – took 11 minutes.

MIRANDA IS ONLY 472KM (293 MILES) ACROSS. THAT'S SMALLER THAN THE ASTEROID VESTA. MIRANDA WOULD EASILY FIT WITHIN THE BORDERS OF THE US STATE OF ARIZONA.

INFLATE THE MATTRESS!

You wouldn't need a bungee rope, or even a parachute, to dive off a cliff on Miranda. In fact, neither of them would really work. If you were brave enough to try it, an inflatable airbag or mattress at the base of the cliff ought to be enough to cushion your fall. On Miranda, everyone can be Felix Baumgartner for a day.

THE LOW GRAVITY ON MIRANDA – LESS THAN ONE PERCENT OF EARTH'S – COULD MAKE YOUR BUNGEE JUMPS VERY GENTLE INDEED. JUST ENJOY THE VIEW!

Surfing Titan

As you now know, the first liquid waves have been detected on the surface of another world. Your data has confirmed that Saturn's giant moon, Titan, has lakes and seas. However, as these bodies of liquid are made of fuel-like substances – rather than water – would it be possible to go surfing in the Saturn system?

Titan has a 30-year seasonal cycle. Its northern region will next have a summer solstice (its longest sunlit day) in 2017.

There's not enough oxygen on Earth to burn all the highly flammable methane on Titan!

Earth's Tides

On Earth, the ocean tides are caused by the gravitational pull of the Moon and the Sun – in association with the rotation of the Earth. The Moon is significantly closer to us than the Sun is, so its gravity exerts the greater pull on our ocean as it orbits the Earth. The ocean bulges and dips in response to the movement of the Earth and Moon, and we see this as high and low tides.

Wave Power

Waves of all shapes and sizes roll into beaches on Earth at any time, night or day. Waves can travel across entire ocean basins – so, the waves at a beach you're standing on might have been started by weather conditions many thousands of kilometres away. The most familiar ocean waves are driven by winds, which in turn are caused by the Sun heating the planet.

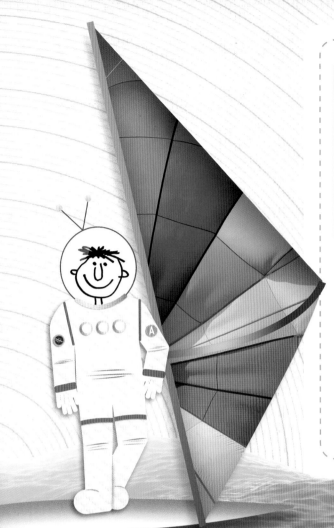

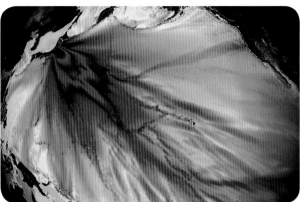

Predicting Tsunamis

Scientists say the next eruption of the Cumbre Vieja volcano – on the Canary Islands, in the Atlantic Ocean – will trigger a mega-tsunami (a sequence of gigantic waves). The volcano's western flank will fall into the sea, producing waves 1000m (3280ft) high – at first – with a height of around 50m (165ft) when they reach the other side of the Atlantic. Try surfing those!

Surf's Up On Titan?

Titan's atmosphere is also very windy. Down at the surface level, though, the winds are fairly weak – so the waves on the lakes and seas are more like ripples, approximately 2cm (0.8in) high. It's possible, however, that the moon has seasonal changes, bringing stormier conditions. This could create 1m-high (3.3ft-high) waves, good enough for windsurfing!

Rocket-Fuel Waves

Titan's lakes and seas contain fuel-like substances – liquid methane and ethane (see pages 116–117). In fact, the moon has 40 times the estimated reserves of natural oil and gas on Earth. Methane is not toxic (poisonous), but the human body isn't really designed to swim in it. Any future Titan-surfers would have to wear some kind of protective wetsuit!

09 LOOKING FOR LIFE

Before you look for life beyond the Earth, think about exactly what life is. Your onboard computer says that scientists have pondered this question for many centuries. It's a question that's harder to answer than you think. How can you tell if something is alive? That's the aim of your current mission: to find out the conditions for life on Earth, and then explore where else in the Solar System life might survive.

Kit Checklist:

☐ Command module
☐ Powerful microscope
☐ Cryobot
  (robotic ice-drilling probe)
☐ Landing rovers
☐ Vapour-sampling probe
☐ Onboard microbe analyser

BEYOND THE FROST LINE

Watch out for our Solar System's 'frost line', which lies somewhere in the midst of the Asteroid Belt, in between Mars and Jupiter. Beyond this point, the temperatures are truly freezing – but the conditions in some places out there may still be good enough for life to evolve. On your journey, you will explore the possibilities.

The distances in space are so vast, it may be that artifical life, such as robots, will be key to finding natural life.

IT'S TIME TO RETURN TO EARTH — FOR NOW!

WHEREVER YOU ARE ON YOUR JOURNEY — WHETHER BASKING IN THE WARMTH OF YOUR HOME PLANET OR EXPLORING THE ICY REGIONS AROUND JUPITER AND SATURN — REMEMBER THAT THE SUN IS CRUCIAL TO LIFE.

VENUS

EARTH

TOO HOT!

MARS

JUST RIGHT

TOO COLD!

THE GOLDILOCKS ZONE

Our planet sits right in the middle of the Solar System's 'Goldilocks Zone', where it is 'not too hot' and 'not too cold' for life. On Earth, the surface temperature is 'just right' – at an average of 15°C (59°F).

WHAT MAKES LIFE?

Even though you live on Earth, you may not be familiar with just how many different life forms there are upon it. So you will need to use your spacecraft's computer to do a bit of detective work. Life on this planet is extraordinarily varied – from tiny, simple organisms to large and very complex ones. However, no matter how different these living things may look, they ALL have some very important things in common.

THE FEATURES OF LIFE:

All life forms on Earth share these characteristics:

1. Life forms are made up of tiny cells.
2. Life forms grow and use energy.
3. Life forms respond to their surroundings.
4. Life forms reproduce (make copies of) themselves.
5. Life forms change over time. They 'evolve'.

MADE OF CELLS

Your computer explains that plants and animals are made up of one or more cells. Cells are the basic building blocks of all life. Some organisms, such as bacteria, are made up of just a single cell (unicellular). Others, such as human beings, are made up of many cells (multicellular). All living things are organised in what we call a 'cellular' construction.

ENERGISED

All life uses energy. Space explorers do this with food. You convert the chemicals and energy in your food into stuff that your cells can use. Plants and animals need energy to keep the functions of life going. One of these functions is growth. Organisms get bigger and more complicated – from offspring (baby) to adult – in an organised way.

REPRODUCTIVE

Your computer is now telling you about two different types of reproduction – the processes by which living things make new copies of themselves. If organisms make copies from just a single parent, then it's called 'asexual' reproduction. If they make copies from two parents, it's known as 'sexual' reproduction. A chemical called DNA – contained in all living cells – contains the unique instructions needed to build and repair a life form.

RESPONSIVE

All living things respond to their surroundings. Tiny, single-celled creatures respond to chemicals in their environment. Many-celled organisms tend to move around more, so they have developed complicated senses – such as seeing, hearing and smelling – which process information about the world around them. Other types of responses can be small and simple, such as a plant turning its leaves towards the Sun.

EVOLVING

Plants and animals 'evolve'. This means that they change and adapt over time due to the challenges presented by the environment in which they live. The most successful living organisms are those that are able to become better at living in their surroundings. Their DNA passes on their 'successful' characteristics to later generations, while the less successful features – and organisms – tend to disappear.

Where Life Started

Since you've been back on Earth, you've been spending a lot of time in the oceans, which is where life on Earth may have started. But now it's time to plant your feet back on dry land and investigate the full range of ingredients that go into cooking up living organisms. You can also look at all the other places where life may have begun.

P

H

O_2

C

Absorbs Carbon Dioxide

Absorbs Sunlight for Energy

Produces oxygen

Drinks Water

Organic Material

The stuff that makes up living matter is known as 'organic' material. All matter is made of tiny particles called atoms, and different types of atoms are called elements. Some of these chemical elements – including carbon (C), hydrogen (H), oxygen (O_2) and phosphorus (P) – combine to make living, organic material. One such chemical combination is DNA, the most essential ingredient for life's functions.

Water and Energy

Your computer says that for life to exist on Earth, water is vital. Biologists believe that water carries the chemicals of life to and fro. Other liquids may act as hosts for life, such as methane on Titan. Energy, too, is an important factor. The energy for most living things on this planet comes from the Sun's light. Plants convert this energy into food, which animals eat to get energy into their bodies.

Ice Caps

Life can survive the most extreme locations. Earth's two icy polar oceans are very unwelcoming places, and yet more than 12,000 species have been found there. So was this the starting point for living organisms? One example of extreme polar life is a microscopic, eight-legged creature called a water bear, or tardigrade. Water bears can survive in temperatures ranging from -272°C (-458°F) to 151°C (304°F). In 2007, tardigrades (taken on board a shuttle) were put into the airless environment of space to see if they could also withstand the lack of water and oxygen, as well as the extreme temperatures and levels of solar radiation. They passed the test!

Now you've studied the ingredients and locations of living things, it's time to consider the possibility of life on other moons and planets. First stop, Mars!

Vent Life

As water is essential for life, biologists think life could have begun in the seas, deep down around the planet's hydrothermal vents (see pages 84–85). The vents release hot water, together with a cocktail of super-heated minerals. The minerals in the water allow bacteria to thrive. The bacteria convert the minerals into food for other animals. So, the creatures here do not need sunlight to survive – and some experts believe that life on Earth began in these deep-sea ecosystems.

Life On Land

As a space explorer, you are a fine example of a 'limbed' animal. So, you may like to hear that limbed creatures – animals with arms, legs and so on – started in the seas. Tetrapod ('four-footed') animals like you evolved from lobe-finned fishes, which began to come ashore around 375 million years ago.

MARTIANS

While examining the data from your previous mission to Mars, you know that the conditions for life may be good. Astronomers have studied the surface of the Red Planet through their telescopes for well over a hundred years. The key piece of evidence you need is the range of temperatures on Mars… **Can you find out exactly how hot and cold it gets?**

20km (12.4miles)
above surface

Thermal
report

-17.2
-20
-85
-90
-107

Vapour levels
75.7485.9302

TEMPERATURE RANGE

Mars lies perilously close to the 'frost line' that we warned you about in your mission briefing! As your robotic rover has just reminded you, the average temperature on Mars is -55°C (-67°F). Surface temperatures may get as high as 20°C (68°F) at noon on the equator, and as low as -153°C (-243°F) at the poles.

THIN ATMOSPHERE

Scientists think that the disappearance of the Martian water is mainly down to its atmosphere. The planet's atmosphere is very thin, too thin to keep in the heat. So, over time, Mars became so cold that its liquid water disappeared. A lot of it may have been vaporised (boiled away) by the Sun's radiation.

WATERY ATMOSPHERE

So, you programme your orbiting probe to study this atmosphere in more detail, and it sends back some surprising data… At heights of 20–50 km (12.5–31 miles) above the surface, there's 10 to 100 times more water vapour than scientists expected. This could be the way Mars has been losing its water. When the Sun's radiation hits the water vapour, the water splits into oxygen and hydrogen and is lost into space.

MARTIAN CANALS

In the late 1800s, the idea of life on Mars was a popular one. Some scientists thought that marks on the planet's surface were canals, purposefully constructed by Martians to channel water from place to place. For example, they reckoned alien beings were using the canals to bring water from the polar caps down to the dry areas near to the equator. Eventually, astronomers realised that the 'canals' were deep, natural features in the landscape.

LIFE UNDERGROUND

Water is not the only condition for life. Life must also be protected from a hostile environment. In the past, Mars had a magnetic field, which protected the planet from cosmic and solar rays. So maybe Martian microbes are hiding deep under the crust in cracks and caves made by volcanoes, sheltering from today's much harsher surface conditions.

Antarctic ice sheet, Earth

Northern polar cap, Mars

POLAR WATER

Using your rover and orbiter, you take new readings of the Martian surface. The ice caps at the north and south poles consist mainly of water ice, but there is also frozen carbon dioxide on their surfaces. The northern polar cap is about 1000km (620 miles) across during the northern Martian summer, and contains about 1.6 million cubic km (0.4 million cubic miles) of ice. The biggest single mass of ice on Earth is the Antarctic ice sheet, which contains about 26.5 million cubic km (6.36 million cubic miles) of water ice. So that gives you an idea of how much more watery the Earth is, compared to Mars!

Europa's Oceans

Your spacecraft has made a gravitational slingshot around Mars, and presently you find yourself back in the Jupiter system. On your last visit here, you sent a probe to drill through Europa's icy crust, down into the murky depths of what we think might be seas below it. Now it's time to check on the probe's progress.

Hubble

OCEAN BELOW

The jets on Saturn's moon Enceladus contain ice and dust particles, as well as water (see pages 62–63). But your console analysis says that only water has been detected in Europa's jets. If predictions are right, Europa's suspected seas contain twice the amount of water found across Earth! Time to take a closer look at what your probe uncovered.

WARM OR COLD?

THE PROBE HAS DETECTED THE CHEMICALS NEEDED FOR LIFE IN EUROPA'S SEAS.

The average temperature of the ocean is chilly – at about -160°C (-256°F) – but Jupiter's gravity produces tides on Europa, similar to the giant planet's stretching effects on Io (see pages 88–89). This 'tidal flexing' produces the water jets that Hubble spotted. The effect of these tides is mainly felt towards the moon's core. This may mean temperatures could be warm enough – in places – to support pockets of life.

Alien Vents

The existence of life on this moon depends on whether Europa, like Earth, has hydrothermal vents (see pages 84–85 and 108–109), which would provide the energy and material needed for life in its alien seas. So far, however, your probe has found no signs of the dark, mineral-rich waters that are created by such vents. But the Europan ocean is HUGE, so there's plenty more sea left to explore!

EUROPA'S JETS

The Hubble Space Telescope spied 200km-high (125 mile-high) jets of liquid vapour erupting from Europa's south pole. As with Saturn's moon Enceladus (see pages 62–63), this may be evidence that stuff from a sub-surface ocean is being sprayed directly into space. So, you now guide your orbiting craft through the misty vapour, to try and pick up a distant uplink signal from the probe you programmed to drill down into the crust.

FIND THE WATER

As you leave the Jupiter system, heading into deeper space, you pick up a signal from NASA's Cassini spacecraft. It has detected a large body of salty water beneath the surface of Enceladus, a world you encountered on your first tour of the Solar System's most interesting moons. But how has the spacecraft made this discovery without actually landing on Enceladus?

LIFE ELEMENTS

The saltwater ocean isn't the only thing that's got the scientists excited about Enceladus. The water on the moon is in contact with the moon's rocky core. That means the elements useful for life, such as phosphorus and sulphur, will leak into the ocean and – hopefully – help organic life to get going in the water.

WHAT SORTS OF LIFE MIGHT WE FIND IN THE DEPTHS OF ENCELADUS'S OCEANS?

WATER: FACTORY OF LIFE

Scientists believe water is a factory of life, giving chemicals the right kind of environment in which to combine and thrive. The elements hydrogen and oxygen make up water. On their own, they are explosive. But together they combine to make the safest of materials, one that is unchanging over a wide range of temperatures. That's why space agencies, such as NASA, always 'follow the water' when they go looking for life on other planets.

Deep Water

The uncrewed Cassini spacecraft (see pages 66–67) has measured the gravitational field of Enceladus while making 100km-high (62 mile-high) flybys of the moon. The measurements suggest that there may be a 10km-deep ocean – larger than Lake Superior in the USA – lurking beneath the icy surface of the moon's southern pole. This massive body of salty water may even extend all the way to the north.

Testing Samples

There's only one way to be sure about life on Enceladus – and that's to send a mission out to take samples of the water vapour in the moon's plumes (see pages 62–63) and bring them back to Earth. That way, scientists can properly test the liquid for the presence of organic chemicals – or even tiny, microbial forms of organic life.
Yes, that's right – little aliens!

Organic Titan

Approaching Titan, you hope the haze and the clouds will break open into a gap, if only a few kilometres across, so that you might spy some little detail of its hidden surface. But its atmosphere is still as dense and stubborn as you found it to be on your tour of the moons. You'll have to rely on the probe you sent down on that earlier mission.

An Early Earth?

Like Earth, Titan's atmosphere is mostly nitrogen. But unlike Earth, Titan has only small traces of oxygen and water. Instead, liquid methane plays the same role on Titan that water plays on Earth. Scientists think that Titan is like the Earth was in its early days, billions of years ago, before primitive life forms started to release oxygen into our planet's atmosphere.

A Living World?

Scientists think Titan could evolve to be more like the Earth. At the higher peaks on Titan, energy from the Sun sparks chains of organic reactions involving an element called carbon. The presence of carbon is important, because this element is the basis of all known life on Earth. BUT… at roughly -179.5°C (-291°F), Titan is just too cold for life. In the distant future, however – when the Sun swells up to become a 'red giant' star – Titan's temperatures will rise. This might allow liquid water to form, which in turn might allow life forms to evolve there.

THE AIR ON TITAN IS VERY THICK AND THE GRAVITY IS LOW. SO, ALL A SPACE EXPLORER NEEDS TO FLY IS A SMALL PAIR OF WINGS, ABOUT 3M (10FT) ACROSS, POWERED BY YOUR MUSCLES! YOU COULD SOAR LIKE A BIRD OVER THE SEAS AND LAKES OF TITAN.

RAIN AND ROCK

The latest weather report from your ground-based probe (see pages 66–67) shows up more of those clouds of a natural gas called methane. When the clouds get too heavy, they release a downpour of 'fuel-like' rain. The raindrops you see are 50 per cent larger than those on Earth, and they fall to the ground much more slowly – a bit like snowfall. This 'petrochemical' rain erodes (wears away) the landscape, creating valleys and lakes. It's a good job there isn't any oxygen in the atmosphere, as it would react with these fuel-like chemicals and cause them to blow up!

10 STAYING OVER

How hard would it be to live in space? Since the early days of space exploration, writers and scientists have imagined our future in the cosmos. In many ways, colonisation of other worlds is the ultimate aim of spaceflight. But how might we turn hostile planets into places we could inhabit?

a

Kit Checklist:

☐ Ticket to the ISS
☐ Lunar Surface Mobility suit
☐ Lunar Roving Vehicle (LRV)
☐ Earth Return Vehicle (ERV)
☐ Mars Roving Vehicle (MRV)
☐ Asteroid Landing Probe

As NASA's mission statement says...

"If we humans want to survive... we must ultimately populate other planets."

The idea of colonising space goes back centuries, but one of the first accounts of a space colony was in Edward Everett Hale's 1869 book, 'Brick Moon', which described how a colony in space could happen by accident!

Human activities have destroyed many of the beautiful, delicate environments on Earth. This has had an impact on the natural habitats and migration routes of animals, leading to the extinction of certain species. It has also caused the erosion (wearing away) of the soil where plants make their homes. We need to learn from our mistakes on Earth and be more careful with the way we treat the other worlds of the Solar System.

Martian living: Factoids

#1 Scientists have found that lichen plants can survive in Mars-like conditions.

#2 Life-related chemicals, such as methane and formaldehyde, have been found in the Martian atmosphere.

THE SPACE STATIONS AND WHO MADE THEM

a SKYLAB (NASA)

b ISS (GLOBAL)

c MIR (FKA)

Earthlings in Space

The International Space Station, or ISS, has allowed us to keep humans in space, constantly, since the year 2000. The experience of being in orbit for so long has taught us much about how we must adapt to the conditions of life in space. But how did we get to this point of being in space every day? And what lessons did we learn on the way?

The Huntsville Times

Man Enters Space

'So Close, Yet So Far,' Sighs Cape

U.S. Had Hoped For Own Launch

Hobbs Admits

Soviet Offic Orbits Glo' In 5-Ton S

Maximum Height Reported As 188

Animals In Space

Before humans dared to venture into space, animals were sent to see if they could cope with spaceflight. So, the first astronauts were actually fruit flies, sent up to a height of 109km (68 miles) – past what we call the 'edge of space' – to test the effects of radiation on their bodies at high altitudes. Two spiders – named Gladys and Esmeralda – also made a trip, to study the effects of microgravity on their behaviour.

Human Endurance

Another vital test for spaceflight is 'high-G training'. This training prepares humans for the high levels of acceleration ('G') they must endure in space travel. The training, using G-force simulators, is designed to stop astronauts passing out when G-forces move the blood away from the brain.

Early Pioneers

On 12 April 1961, Russian cosmonaut Yuri Gagarin became the first human to journey into space, when his Vostok spacecraft completed an orbit of the Earth. Valentina Tereshkova became the first woman in space on 16 June 1963. As Tereshkova was not a cosmonaut, she also became the first civilian to fly in space. As she orbited, she sang – so she was also the first person to *sing* in space!

> LAA-LA LAAAA LAH!

Space Stations

By the 1970s, astronauts were living successfully in orbiting space stations. The Russian Salyut craft, launched in 1971, was the world's first crewed station. NASA launched their Skylab space station in 1973. Another Russian station, Mir, set a new record in 1994–95, when cosmonaut Valeri Polyakov spent 437 days on board – setting the longest time continuously spent in space.

The ISS

Today's International Space Station has also made it clear that humans can live for long periods in low-Earth orbit. The first ISS crew (of three people) arrived in November 2000. They stayed on board for 136 days, until the next 'long-duration team' arrived. Research and experiments conducted on board have taught us how to be self-sufficient and look after ourselves in space. Scientists can use this data to plan for a colony on the Moon.

ISS FACTOIDS

#1 In its first 10 years, the ISS completed 57,361 orbits of the Earth, covering 2.4 billion km (1.5 billion miles), and was visited by 204 people.

#2 The sunlit ISS can be seen in our dark skies, in the hours after sunset or before sunrise. It appears as a slow-moving, bright white dot.

Lunar Living

The Moon has been a target of colonisation for many years. It is on our cosmic doorstep, within easy reach of Earth. This closeness might enable colonists, living and working on the Moon, to exchange goods for the things they need from Earth. The Moon is also a great place to set up powerful telescopes, and a stepping-stone for further human exploration.

FOR SALE

SORRY WE'RE *closed*

Protecting the Moon

In the early days of space travel, national governments paid the costs. Space missions were mostly launched in the spirit of exploration for all mankind. Today, space travel is big business, with billions of pounds being spent on it every year. Governments will have to make sure that the Moon is not ruined by reckless commercial missions intent on stripping it of its minerals and natural resources.

The Apollo Missions

NASA's Apollo missions, of 1969–72, put a total of 12 human beings on the Moon, and tested the challenges of lunar living. Each mission was longer than the previous one, to explore the Moon further and see how well the astronauts could cope while conducting different types of experiments. The Apollo programme also taught us how to transport large items of equipment and materials to another world.

The Challenges

Visiting the Moon is one thing, but living there won't be easy. There are huge temperature swings, from 134ºC (273ºF) at noon to -170ºC (-274ºF) at night. The surface is constantly blasted by micrometeorites and cosmic rays. To survive this bombardment, colonists might have to live underground in 'lava tubes' – long, natural caves formed by the flow of magma in the past.

Lunar Farming

A number of nations still hope to put humans back on the Moon. One plan is to put a farm at its northern pole. A farm here would receive eight hours of sunlight each day, throughout the lunar summer. The farm could have a special protection from the fierce solar radiation, and a safe environment for insects for pollination. But even so, a farm measuring 100m by 100m (328ft by 328ft) would not be able to feed 100 people.

Food And Water

The availability of food and water is another challenge for colonising the Moon. Scientists believe that water is hidden in the soil at the southern lunar pole. Special machinery would be needed to extract the water from the ground. Growing plants will also be difficult. The nights can be long and cold, and the daylight is bright and harsh, as there is no atmosphere on the Moon to reduce and scatter the Sun's radiation. There are also no insects there to pollinate the flowers!

Transforming Mars

As you found on your previous missions to the Red Planet, Mars has much in common with our own world. Unfortunately, though, it lacks some of the crucial things we need to live, such as warm temperatures and liquid water. So how would human colonists go about transforming Mars to fix these crucial differences?

Earth Return Vehicle

Before any colonists arrive, an uncrewed Earth Return Vehicle (ERV) could be sent to Mars. The ERV would contain a nuclear reactor, which would power a unit to make fuel, using material found in the Martian atmosphere. Two years later, a human crew could then touch down near the ERV. The colonists would stay for about 18 months, exploring the planet until they returned to Earth using the ERV and the fuel it had prepared. The crew would be replaced by another team, and a string of Mars bases would be set up.

Roaming Mars

At first, the brave colonists would depend on supplies arriving from Earth. The Martian bio-domes, where they'd live, would let in sunlight and screen out the harmful solar rays. Spacesuits would not be needed, as they could roam around in oxygen masks and protective clothing. This way, people could leave their domes and set out to build other domed villages and farms.

DIFFICULT CONDITIONS

Some scientists believe that the next generation of space explorers should skip the Moon and head straight for Mars. However, as on the Moon, a Martian colony would have to overcome many challenging conditions – such global dust-storms and powerful solar radiation. To release water onto the surface, colonists would have to find a way to melt the planet's polar ice into a sea 12m (40ft) deep, covering much of the planet. **A huge task!**

WARMING A WORLD

The entire planet would need to be transformed, or 'terraformed', before we could grow things in its soil. Special units would pump gases, such as methane and ammonia, into the atmosphere. The gases would absorb solar energy and warm the planet, triggering the release of carbon dioxide from the soil and ice caps. The carbon dioxide in the atmosphere would help to absorb and spread out the heat from the Sun, which would cause the polar ice to melt and form liquid seas.

FROM RED TO BLUE..?

After several decades of terraforming, Mars might look as blue and watery as Earth does. Within a century, it could be terraformed into an oxygen-rich environment, supporting a human colony, some of whom may dream of travelling further on to the remote corners of the Solar System – and beyond.

Mining the Belt

In the midst of the Asteroid Belt sits Ceres, a dwarf planet that is one-third the mass of the whole Belt. The surface of Ceres is a little larger than Argentina, a South American country on Earth. Could Ceres be the base and transport hub for the entire Belt, allowing the asteroids to be explored and mined for their minerals?

Pit Stop

Stepping Stones

The Asteroid Belt is full of natural resources. Each rocky body contains tonnes and tonnes of minerals. These could become very valuable to us Earthlings as our global population increases and our own resources begin to run out. But could we really use Ceres as a base for mining, to extract materials from these big space lumps? Only time will tell.

Asteroid Sampling

After travelling for two years, NASA's OSIRIS-REx spacecraft will meet with asteroid 101955 Bennu, and begin to map its surface from 5km (3 miles) away. The mapping will last for 505 days, after which the mission team will select a site where the spacecraft's robotic arm can grab a sample of the asteroid – and return it to Earth for examination.

Money Belt

If we went to Ceres to set up a mining base, and then started drilling for materials on the surrounding asteroids, it would mean we wouldn't have to do the same thing on the Moon. The rewards in the Asteroid Belt are enormous. The value of the platinum-group metals alone – in a single small worldlet – is estimated at trillions of pounds. A handful of private companies plan to mine near-Earth asteroids by around 2020, but it is not yet clear how they will return the materials to the Earth's surface.

The Dawn Mission

NASA's Dawn mission shows that the Asteroid Belt is quite an easy area to navigate. The Dawn spacecraft will visit Ceres and a very large asteroid called Vesta. Two of Dawn's main aims are to discover how these two small worlds followed very different paths of evolution, and to better understand their make-up.

PREPARING OURSELVES

Whether the mission is to colonise another planet, begin mining in outer space or turn an asteroid into a city – us humans have got to get organised. We need to consider new fuels, new types of propulsion and new types of spacecraft. We also need to prepare ourselves both physically and mentally.

ARE YOU READY TO COLONISE THE SOLAR SYSTEM? ARE YOU SURE...??

SPACE SETTLEMENTS

In 1975, a group of professors met for 10 weeks to design space colonies. They recommended colonies that travelled in orbit around planets or moons. These wheel-like habitats were designed to be about 1.6km (1 mile) in diameter. The colonists would live inside a tubular structure, which would rotate to simulate the effects of gravity, and use mirrors to harness solar power.

ION DRIVES

Scientists have also looked into the possibility of building spacecraft that are pushed along by nuclear power. Nuclear fuels are lighter and more efficient than conventional fuel, and could take a spacecraft much further in space – but they are not always safe to use. Another option would be to use an ion engine, in which electrically charged particles are channelled into a beam. This beam creates pulses of thrust, which could push the spacecraft in the opposite direction.

MARS LOOKS A BIT RUSTY RIGHT NOW, BUT IT'LL BE NICE AND BLUE WHEN IT'S TERRAFORMED!

MARS500 MEMBERS CELEBRATING THE CHINESE NEW YEAR

Recreating Mars

NASA's Mars Exploration Program aims to find out whether Mars can become a home for humans. To study Mars-like conditions right here on Earth, scientists from the European Space Agency (ESA) have created a 'Mars Yard' – a landscape that recreates the Martian terrain and climate. The better we know Mars, the more prepared we'll be when we attempt to colonise it in the future.

Mars500

The Mars500 project – carried out by Russia, China and the ESA – prepared people for these very long bouts of isolation on flights to Mars. Between 2007 and 2011, volunteers lived and worked in a pretend spacecraft, an ascent-descent craft, and on a specially created 'Martian' surface. The different crews lived in isolation – without fresh food, sunlight or fresh air. They had very limited contact with the outside world.

(11) DEEP SPACE

If space explorers ventured beyond the Solar System, what would they find? A revolution is happening in astronomy. Scientists have studied distant stars for centuries, but only lately have they found evidence of the thousands of planets that exist in orbit around them. It's time to look at these exotic stars and planets – the possible destinations for future exploration.

Kit Checklist:

- [ ] Deep-space command module
- [ ] Space observatory
- [ ] Catalogue of star types
- [ ] Catalogue of exoplanet types
- [ ] Exoplanet analysis probe
- [ ] Stasis chamber (for very long journeys)

L.P.K
STAR TYPES VOL 1

STAR TYPES Volume 1
Star Types: Volume 2
Star Types: Complete

The Kepler observatory is named after a German mathematician and astronomer called Johannes Kepler. He was the first person to work out the maths behind the motion of the planets.

STASIS CONTROL

BPM	: 90
O2	: 756
BF	: 100%
LF	: 100%
KF	: 98%
BP	: 120/80

The Kepler Space Observatory

The Kepler observatory, which orbits the Sun, is searching for exoplanets – planets that lie beyond our own Solar System. It is a highly specialised telescope that focuses on a portion of our galaxy, the Milky Way. The spacecraft's mission is to try and identify planets that orbit their star, or stars, in a habitable location (that is not too hot and not too cold). Gradually, it is helping us to estimate the number of stars that may have Earth-like planets in orbit around them.

The Kepler space observatory was launched by NASA on 6 March 2009. NASA later announced that two of the spacecraft's main parts had become disabled. So be prepared. On your way into deeper space, you may be asked to stop at the observatory and make some repairs!

Johannes Kepler (1571–1630)

Star Types

Beyond our Solar System, a space explorer can expect to find systems similar to our own – planets, of varying sizes and types, moving around other suns. In future generations, these other systems will be explored in more depth, by robotic missions. Humans will want to find out exactly how typical our Sun and Solar System are.

STAR CLOUDS

Stars form from huge clouds of gassy material. The gas clumps together to form a young, glowing star at the centre. A revolving disc of gassy and dusty material circulates around it.

AVERAGE STARS

Stars come in different sizes and masses. Mass is a measure of the amount of gassy material making up the star, and it influences the type of life a star leads. Most stars are Sun-sized or smaller.

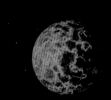

RED GIANT

When stars begin to burn helium, they expand in size to become red giants. In billions of years' time, our Sun will become a red giant, expanding to 200 times its current size.

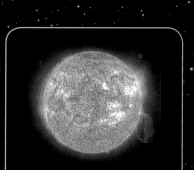

MASSIVE STARS

Large, monster stars are less common. They have shorter lives, counted in millions – rather than billions – of years. This is because they burn up their gassy fuel at a much faster rate.

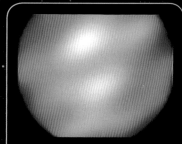

RED SUPERGIANT

When large stars start burning helium they become red supergiants. These are the largest stars in the known Universe, ranging between 200 and 800 times the size of our Sun.

How Stars Evolve

For most of their lives, stars burn hydrogen and convert it into helium. When they run out of hydrogen, they burn the helium instead. Stars never 'die', not exactly. They evolve, which means they become a different type of star over the course of an extremely long period of time – usually billions of years. The way in which they evolve depends on how massive they are to begin with.

PLANETARY NEBULA

After millions of years as a red giant, the star shrinks again. It pushes off its outer layers to create a 'planetary' nebula. These 'shells' of gas are usually very beautiful.

WHITE DWARF

Within the planetary nebula, the hot core of the star still remains. Its own gravity has caused it to shrink, and it will stay as a 'white dwarf' for rest of its life.

BLACK HOLE

After exploding, VERY large stars keep on shrinking. If they're massive enough, their gravity attracts everything in their neighbourhood of space. Nothing, not even light, can escape this gravitational effect – so these regions turn into black holes.

SUPERNOVA

Massive stars explode! When they run out of fuel to burn, they collapse in on themselves and explode in an enormous burst of light – more light than an average star gives out in its entire lifetime!

NEUTRON STAR

Less massive large stars eventually become highly dense, enormously compacted 'neutron' stars. The density of these stars is similar to the mass of a large aircraft squashed down into a tiny grain of sand!

Exoplanets

Planets beyond our Solar System are called exoplanets. Thousands of very real worlds have already been found. A recent estimate from NASA's Kepler telescope suggests there may be 40 billion Earth-like planets in our Galaxy alone. Although there's no place like home, it's exciting to learn about these wonderful worlds.

EARTH × 6

Gliese 667Cc

Gliese 667C is the name of a small, 'red dwarf' star (see pages 136–137). One of the planets orbiting it, known as Gliese 667Cc, is about five times the mass of the Earth, and may have seas on its surface. There are actually three stars, in total, in this particular system. The starlight that Gliese 667Cc receives, overall, is probably about 90 per cent of what we get on Earth.

Gliese 1214b

Gliese 1214b, also called GJ 1214b, is known as a 'super-Earth'. It is around six times larger than Earth, but it has much less mass than the gas giants of our Solar System. Gliese 1214b might be an ocean planet, with its entire surface covered by seas. Scientists say that its atmosphere is likely to be rich in water.

Kepler-11f

The Kepler-11 is a Sun-like star, slightly larger than ours. It has more planets around it than we've seen in any other exoplanet system so far. Five of the six Kepler-11 planets orbit very close to their star. They are nearer to their sun than Mercury is to our Sun. Kepler-11f is a super-Earth, 2.3 times the mass of our own planet.

Kepler 186f

Kepler 186f is the most Earth-like planet we've discovered to date. It's part of a five-planet system that orbits a cool dwarf star, about 500 light years away from Earth. It's a rocky planet, like the Earth, and it appears to have a range of temperatures that would hold water in its liquid state. If that's true, life could exist there.

Gliese 581g

This planet, Gliese 581g, is the sixth planet discovered orbiting the red dwarf star Gliese 581, which is about 20 light years from Earth. Gliese 581g is thought to be in the middle of its habitable zone, making it one of the most Earth-like 'Goldilocks planets' (see pages 104–105). Potentially, life forms could thrive there.

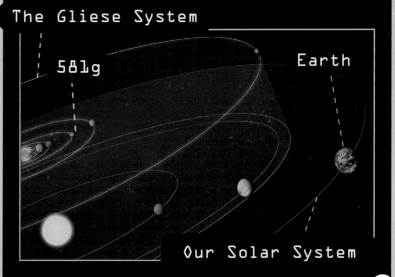

DATA PANEL:
Sister Systems

The Gliese System

581g

Earth

Our Solar System

TWILIGHT WORLDS

In our Milky Way Galaxy, 80 per cent of the stars are red dwarfs. These kind of stars are small and dim, but astronomers believe that Earth-like planets are very common in the habitable zones around them. There may be about one hundred such 'Earths' in the Sun's immediate neighbourhood. A deeper investigation is needed!

Red Dwarf Stars

Red dwarfs are smaller than our Sun, ranging from around one per cent to 50 per cent of the Sun's mass. They're also cooler, and much dimmer, with a surface temperature of about 3725°C (6740°F) – about 1780°C (3235°F) cooler than the Sun's surface. So, although they are very common, they cannot be seen from Earth with the naked eye.

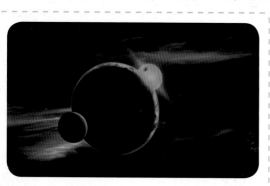

Stable Systems

A star's lifespan depends on its mass. Compared to the Sun's estimated life of 10 billion years, a red dwarf that is half the Sun's mass will live for 56 billion years. Any planet orbiting a red dwarf, sitting in the 'Goldilocks (habitable) zone', would therefore be able to enjoy the heat and light from this star for a very long time – enough time for life to evolve!

ASTRONOMERS RECKON THERE ARE UP TO 400 BILLION STARS IN OUR MILKY WAY GALAXY. SO, UP TO 320 BILLION OF THOSE ARE RED DWARFS - AND UP TO 12 PER CENT OF THE RED DWARFS MAY HAVE EARTH-LIKE WORLDS AROUND THEM!

THAT'S UP TO 40 BILLION PLANETS THAT COULD BE JUST LIKE EARTH!

A

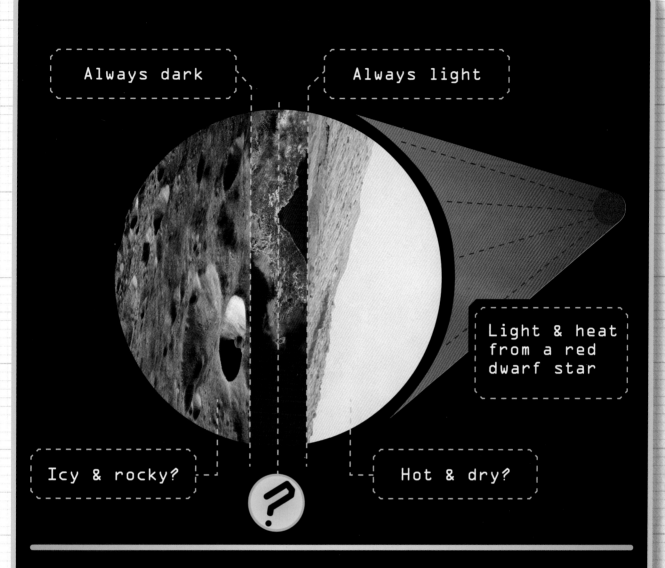

Always dark

Always light

Light & heat from a red dwarf star

Icy & rocky?

Hot & dry?

LOCKED BY GRAVITY

Our Moon is 'locked' in orbit by the Earth's gravity, so we always see the same side of the Moon's surface. The same is true of exoplanets in the habitable zones of red dwarf stars. One half of the exoplanet is in eternal daylight, the other in eternal night.

CONTRASTING CONDITIONS

Red dwarf exoplanets would be strange, exotic worlds. On the night-time side, it would be cold enough to freeze the main gases of the atmosphere. But if the planet had an ocean and a thick atmosphere, they would help to circulate heat around to the other side of the planet, making both sides capable of supporting life.

Seeing Double

Imagine exploring a planet that went round not one star, but two. A planet with two suns might seem straight out of science fiction, but many such 'binary' systems exist in deep space – and there are plenty of planets in orbit about them. What would these systems be like?

Binary Stars

Binary star systems consist of two stars, attracted to each other by their gravity, orbiting around a central point in space. Binaries are actually very common – one half of all visible stars belong to binary systems. The time taken for one star to orbit the other ranges from hours to centuries, depending on their mass and the distance between them.

Forming Binaries

When a gas cloud collapsed – because of gravity – to form our Sun, just one star was formed. When many other gas clouds collapse, they break up to form two stars, instead of one. That's the most common way in which binary star systems are formed.

Binary Types

Astronomers have different ways of classifying binary star systems. One type is a 'detached' binary, where there is no physical contact between the two stars. Another type, known as a 'contact' binary, is where the stars are much closer to one another. In contact binaries, the two stars have a greater gravitational effect on each other, which makes them both slightly egg-shaped.

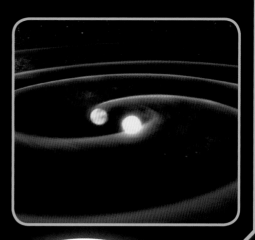

SOMETIMES, A SMALL STAR CAN BE 'CAPTURED' BY THE GRAVITY OF ANOTHER — BUT ASTRONOMERS DON'T THINK THIS IS A VERY COMMON EVENT.

PLANETS IN BINARIES

Kepler-16b is a planet that orbits two stars. Known as a 'circumbinary' planet, astronomers reckon it is a frozen world made up of rock and gas, with roughly the same mass as Saturn. It is about 200 light years from Earth, in a constellation of stars called Cygnus. Kepler-16b orbits its two suns once every 229 days.

NEVER-ENDING DAYLIGHT

Try to imagine living on a planet that goes around two or more stars. It might never get dark, or not very often. What if there was darkness only once every one thousand years or so? How would plants and animals — such as humans — cope with the darkness they had never experienced before?

SPAGHETTIFICATION

It's time to explore the weird and wonderful physics of black holes – regions of space with such high density, and such extreme gravity, that they have a 'warping' effect on everything around them. That includes time, space itself, and any human beings foolish enough to get too close!

BLACK HOLE STARS

Stars that are more massive than average sometimes go into a rather mysterious phase. Just before the explosive, supernova phase of a very massive star (see pages 132–133), the star basically collapses in on itself, or 'implodes'. As all of its matter shrinks down, uncontrollably, a region is created that has an incredible compactness, or density. Nothing nearby, including light, can escape the gravitational grip of this region. A black hole is born.

THE SCIENCE OF SPAGHETTIFICATION

#1

GRAVITY FIELDS

What happens to you near a black hole is all based on gravity fields. According to Albert Einstein (1879-1955), mass warps space. That means that space is curved, wherever there is a mass. Furthermore, space is warped by different amounts in different places.

#2

GRAVITY ON EARTH

Space around Earth is 'warped' more at sea level than it is at the top of high mountains. This is because sea level is closer to the Earth's core - its centre of gravity. So, by the very tiniest amount, your toes experience more gravity than the top of your head does. Your toes are kind of like sea level, while the top of your head is a little like Mount Everest - on a much smaller scale!

#3

GETTING SPAGHETTIFIED

The space near a black hole is HUGELY warped. If you were floating there - with your feet towards the black hole - the gravitational difference between your toes and the top of your head would be unbelievably huge. The overall effect of this massive gravity difference would be this: your body would be stretched out lengthways, like a noodle. The black hole would totally 'spaghettify' you.

?

DO THEY REALLY EXIST?

If these regions of space are perfectly black, giving out no light, how do we know they exist? We don't have any real evidence for black holes – they exist only in theory. But astronomers are looking for telltale signs of their existence. For example, some stars might orbit around a region of space that seems empty, or we astronomers might even witness an object disappearing into 'blackness'.

12 COMING HOME

Whether your return is from Earth's orbit, a mission to the Moon or a lengthier stay on the ISS, you'll have to face the challenges of re-entry and recovery. We have been launching humans into space for more than half a century. In this time, scientists and technicians have worked extremely hard to improve the health and safety of astronauts returning to Earth.

RETRAINING AS AN EARTHLING

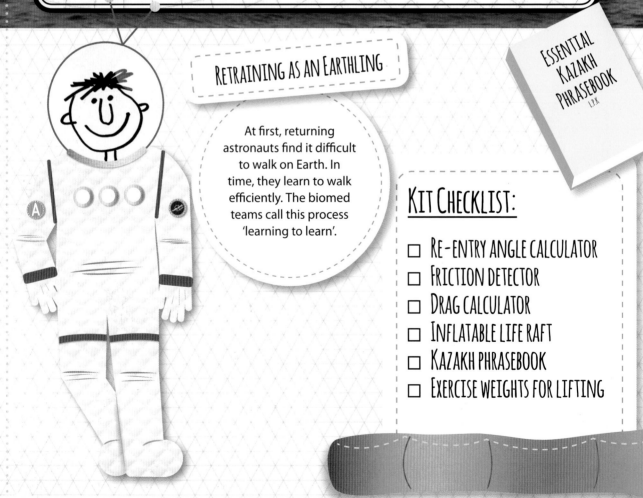

At first, returning astronauts find it difficult to walk on Earth. In time, they learn to walk efficiently. The biomed teams call this process 'learning to learn'.

ESSENTIAL KAZAKH PHRASEBOOK
L.P.K.

KIT CHECKLIST:

☐ RE-ENTRY ANGLE CALCULATOR
☐ FRICTION DETECTOR
☐ DRAG CALCULATOR
☐ INFLATABLE LIFE RAFT
☐ KAZAKH PHRASEBOOK
☐ EXERCISE WEIGHTS FOR LIFTING

Undoing the Dizziness

If you've had a six-month stay on the ISS, get ready for one final challenge. The effects of a long mission are like stepping off a fast-spinning merry-go-round. After a ride on a roller coaster, the effects of motion and dizziness drift away pretty quickly – but after a lengthy stint on a space station, they'll linger for weeks!

Re-entry Angles

Distance:63mi
Speed   :200mps
Gravity :100%
Drag   :75%
Heat   :3000°F
Deploy   :35mi

43.75° East
675° North

RECODING YOUR BRAIN

In space, your senses tell you things are very different, especially when gravity is dramatically reduced. Your brain decodes the new information, makes adjustments and allows you to do the activities you need to perform. When you come home to Earth, the sensory systems need to get used to a normal level of gravity again.

Re-Entry

Launching a spacecraft is one thing. Bringing it back safely is quite another. Re-entering a planet's atmosphere poses different problems, which we've learned how to solve over the years. When your spacecraft jettisons the service module and your command module enters the Earth's atmosphere, it will have to deal with two main forces – gravity and drag.

Gravity Versus Drag

It's gravity that pulls your spacecraft down to Earth. On its own, gravity would cause your spacecraft to fall dangerously quickly – but, thankfully, physics comes to your rescue. The movement of your vehicle through the thickness of the Earth's atmosphere creates friction. This friction causes the spacecraft to experience a resisting force known as 'drag' (see pages 32–33), which slows it down to a safer speed.

DRAG

GRAVITY

It's a Total Drag

Drag is, however, a mixed blessing. As a spacecraft falls through an atmosphere, it is rubbing up against gassy particles. The resulting friction and drag forces create intense heat. Some spacecraft can face re-entry temperatures as great as 1649°C (3000°F)! So, your mission engineers need to bear this in mind when they design and build your spacecraft.

Thermal Protection System

Space shuttles were Reusable Launch Vehicles (RLVs). Instead of using special, one-off materials, the shuttles had a vast, jigsaw-like set of heat-resistant tiles on their bellies. Many of these tiles were reusable, and each one was essential for a safe return. In 2003, the space shuttle Columbia disintegrated during re-entry, because a small number of the tiles had been damaged during the spacecraft's launch.

Apollo Protection

The Apollo mission engineers dealt with the intense heat of re-entry by using vehicles built for one-time use. The command modules were coated with a special material – making up a 'heat shield' – that burned up during re-entry, absorbing much of the heat.

The Apollo heat shield created a 'shock wave' in front of the command module as it re-entered the Earth's atmosphere. This kept the heat at a distance from the spacecraft, and also helped to slow the spacecraft's fall to Earth. Genius!

RETURNING SOYUZ CAPSULES

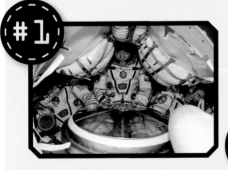

#1

#2

#3

Up to three cosmonauts can return to Earth, from the International Space Station, on board a Soyuz capsule. The commander first pilots the capsule using a joystick that fires eight thrusters on the vehicle. The steering system is then deactivated 15 minutes before landing, when a sequence of four parachutes are deployed.

One after the other, the parachutes dramatically slow the vehicle's descent from 230m (755ft) per second to just 1.5m (5ft) per second – by the time the final, main parachute opens – and then slower still towards the point of touchdown.

The vehicle lands in Kazakhstan, after a total journey time of around 3.5 hours.

SPLASHDOWN!

So, you now know how to return from Earth's orbit, or from nearby places in space, and make a 'dry' landing inside an Earth-return capsule. But what if you're returning from another planet – or from deeper parts of the cosmos – in a larger spacecraft? What is the safest way to get back?

COMMAND MODULE RETURN

During re-entry, the speed of your interplanetary command module should slow down considerably - from 40,000km/h (24,855mph) to around 320km/h (200mph). This is still far too fast for a safe landing, for such a heavy vehicle. So, at around 7km (4.3 miles) above the surface your module's nose cone is ejected and a series of parachutes help to set you gently down into the sea.

WATERY LANDING

Thanks to your parachutes, you'll hit the water at a comfortable 20km/h (12.4mph). That's still quite fast, but it's safe enough for impacting into water. A ring will then inflate around the base of the command module, to turn you the right way up – and keep you afloat so that you send out a radio signal. The rescue team can then find you and pick you up.

CHOPPER RESCUE

Once mission control have received your radio message, they'll either send a boat or a helicopter to collect you. It'll be quite good fun if a chopper comes to get you, as the crew will winch you up into the sky after you have emerged from the command module's hatch. But there's no time for a rest – you'll then need to go for a thorough health check with the biomed team. These tests could last for several weeks.

THE END OF A SPACE STATION

After spending 15 years in orbit around the Earth, the Russian space station Mir (see page 121) reached the end of its service. The station's orbit was deliberately adjusted in March 2001 to bring it down from space. A great deal of the 150-tonne station broke up as it passed through the atmosphere - creating a spectacular firework display in the sky - while the remaining parts plunged into the southern Pacific Ocean. There were as many as 1500 of these pieces, some of them as large as a small car.

MIR'S SPLASHDOWN ENDED A JOURNEY OF MORE THAN 3.2 BILLION KM (2 BILLION MILES) IN SPACE, WHERE IT PLAYED HOST TO 104 COSMONAUTS FROM ALL AROUND THE WORLD.

The After-effects

Maybe you're coming back from a short hop to the Moon. Or maybe you need to recover from the after-effects of a long-haul mission to Mars. Or perhaps it was a six-month stint on the International Space Station. Whatever your mission, once you've made the journey back you'll need to get used to being on Earth again.

Spinal Stretches

A huge reduction in gravity can wreak havoc on an astronaut's body. Take your spine, for example. On Earth, the discs between the vertebrae of your spine are compressed, due to gravity. In space, that compression is gone, which causes the discs to expand. Because of this, astronauts can get as much as 5cm (2in) taller in space!

Vertebrae on Earth

Vertebrae in space

Health & Safety Alert!

WHILE YOU'RE IN SPACE, YOU'LL NEED TO EXERCISE FOR AT LEAST TWO HOURS A DAY – TO KEEP YOUR BONES HEALTHY AND YOUR MUSCLES FROM WASTING AWAY!

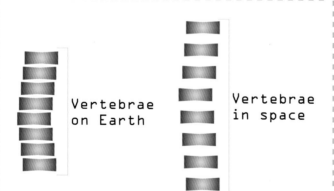

BESIDES EATING AND SLEEPING, WHAT DO ASTRONAUTS SPEND MORE TIME DOING IN SPACE THAN ANYTHING ELSE? EXERCISE! FOR TWO HOURS PER DAY, ON AVERAGE.

Bone mass
-12%

Muscle mass
-40%

Calcium Loss

Astronauts lose calcium (essential to their bones), so once they are back on Earth they may develop conditions similar to osteoporosis – a disease that causes the bones to become more brittle. Calcium loss happens in space because the astronauts do fewer load-bearing exercises than they do on Earth – such as walking, running and lifting things.

Muscle Waste

The longer you stay away, the greater the toll on your body. After five months in orbit above the Earth, an astronaut would typically lose as much as 40 per cent of their muscle mass, and 12 per cent of their bone mass. The muscle loss is the equivalent of a 20-year-old turning into a 60-year-old over a period of five months!

SMELLING AND TASTING

Astronauts love spicy and strong-tasting foods. The air on board spacecraft makes the crew feel as if they've got cold-like symptoms (like on board an aircraft), which means you can't smell and taste things as well. Maybe this is a good thing, as fellow astronauts may have smelly socks! It also means, up in space, a very spicy meal - such as a curry - wouldn't blow your head off, as it would on Earth!

A Different Person

You are lucky. You are special. You are one of the few people who has been into space and experienced the alien conditions there. You've seen our fragile planet hanging in the vastness of space, and you've been to alien worlds to observe them first-hand. How does this make you feel, as a human being from planet Earth?

YOU LAND, AND YOU FEEL THE CRUSHING FORCE OF GRAVITY SUCKING YOU INTO THE GROUND. YOUR HEAD IS SPINNING QUITE A BIT, AS IF THE EARTH IS WOBBLING UNDER YOU WITH HUGE OCEAN CURRENTS.

ONCE YOU'VE LANDED, YOU'LL FEEL THE WEIGHT OF YOUR LIPS AND TONGUE AGAIN. SO YOU MIGHT FIND IT DIFFICULT TO TALK FOR A WHILE!

RECOVERY

In space, you can adapt to microgravity in just a few days. But back on Earth your recovery time depends on the length of your mission. After short flights, your body should recover in about three or four days. But it could take the body up to four weeks to heal after a six-month stay on the ISS. One problem involves the difference in pressure exerted on the eyeballs – about one-fifth of astronauts complain of vision problems after returning to Earth.

RECONDITIONING

Standing and walking are actually major challenges for any astronaut returning to Earth! Getting used to gravity means you'll experience problems with your balance and orientation. Space agencies have come up with specific exercise regimes to help astronauts adjust their head movements and get their fitness and agility back.

WHAT DO ASTRONAUTS TEACH US?

When you look down on Earth from space, the view is wonderful. But the view comes with a realisation that, of all the planets in the Universe, there is only one world that humans can call home.

Astronauts remind us that Earth is our 'spaceship', which transports us around the life-giving Sun. It's easy to take this planet for granted when we're living on it, because it seems so big and so safe. But seeing the planet from space reminds us just how small and fragile the Earth really is.

An astronaut's message to all Earthlings is this: we need to take better care of each other, and extremely good care of our planet.

GLOSSARY

a ALIENS

Life that does not originate on Earth. Alien life has been imagined as microscopic, as well as more monstrous. The study of such extraterrestrial life is known as astrobiology

ATMOSPHERE

A layer of gases that may surround a body of enough mass. Normally that's just planets, but some moons are big enough to have atmospheres too

ATOM

The basic unit of matter. 'Atom' comes from the Greek word 'atomos', which means uncuttable

ASTEROID

A small planetary body in orbit about the sun. The main asteroid belt sits between the orbits of Mars and Jupiter

b BETELGEUSE

A red supergiant star in the constellation of Orion. Betelgeuse is our ninth brightest star, and is 640 light-years away

BIG BANG

A theory of the beginning and evolution of the universe. The theory suggests that the universe began about 13.5 billion years ago

BILLION

One thousand million, or 1,000,000,000

BLACK HOLE

A region of space from which nothing can escape. Black holes may be made by dense matter causing extreme warping of space

c CARBON FOOTPRINT

A measure of the damage done to the environment by the behaviour of a person, object, or organisation

COMET

Small planetary bodies in orbit about the sun. Comets are collections of ice, dust, and rock, and range in size from a few miles to tens of miles across. The main home is thought to be the Oort Cloud

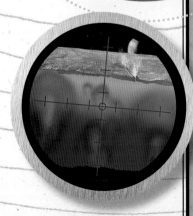

Constellation

An area of the night sky that refers to a pattern of prominent stars, which appear to be close to one another

Crater

A circular dent, made in the surface of a moon or planet, by the high-speed impact of a smaller body

Dwarf Star

A variety of star that is small in size

Earthquake

The sudden release of energy in the Earth's crust that creates tremors, shaking, and can often make cracks in the ground

Escape Velocity

The speed that an object needs to go in order to escape the Earth's gravitational pull on it

Extraterrestrial

Any object or being beyond (extra-) the planet Earth (-terrestrial)

Galaxy

A huge collection of stars, gas and dust bound together by gravity in one system. Galaxies range from dwarfs, with as few as ten million stars, up to giants with one trillion stars. Our own Galaxy is known as the Milky Way

Goldilocks Zone

The zone around a star where it is 'not too hot' and 'not too cold' for life. On Earth, the surface temperature is 'just right' – at an average of 15°C (59°F)

Gravity

The downward force that causes physical objects to fall towards the ground when dropped from a height on Earth

Mass

The mass of a body is a measure of the amount of matter it contains. Weight is a force that results from the action of gravity on a body

Meteor

The visible streak of light that is seen in the sky when a solid object enters the atmosphere of the Earth

Milky Way

The Milky Way, or just Galaxy, is the galaxy in which our solar system is located. It is one of around 170 billion galaxies in the universe

Million

A thousand thousands, or 1,000,000

NASA

NASA is the National Aeronautics and Space Administration. It is an agency of the US government, and is in charge of America's space missions

Orbit

An orbit is the curved path of one body around another, like the orbit of a planet around the sun. The natural phenomenon that keeps bodies in orbit is gravity

Photon(s)

A photon is the basic unit of light. It is an elementary particle, with no mass

Planet

A body orbiting a star that is big enough to be rounded by its own gravity, but not so big that it burns like a star. Planets can be rocky, like Earth, or gas giants, like Jupiter

Solar System

The system of the sun and all bodies bound to it by gravity, including: the four inner rocky planets, the four gassy outer planets, and all the minor bodies, such as asteroids, comets, and dwarf planets, like Pluto

Space

The limitless, 3D extent in which objects and events occur in the universe. Within space, objects have position and direction

Speed of Light

The speed of light is about 300,000 kilometres per second

Star

A massive, luminous ball of gas that is held together by gravity

Stratosphere

The second major layer of Earth's atmosphere, just above the troposphere, and below the mesosphere

Telescope

A device for looking at far away objects. They use lenses or mirrors to make distant things appear far closer

Trillion

One million million, or 1,000,000,000,000

Volcano

An opening in a planet's surface or crust which allows hot magma, ash and gases to escape from below the surface

Vacuum

A volume of space that is approximately empty of matter. In reality, no volume of space can ever be perfectly empty

INDEX

MOUNT EVEREST

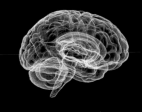

Published in October 2014 by Lonely Planet Publications Pty Ltd
ABN 36 005 607 983
www.lonelyplanet.com
ISBN 978 1 74360 390 1
© Lonely Planet 2014
© Photographs as indicated 2014
Printed in China

Publishing Director	Piers Pickard
Publisher	Mina Patria
Art Director & Visual Direction	Beverley Speight
Author	Mark Brake
Consultant and Editor	Simon Holland
Illustrator & Designer	Emma Jones
Image Researcher	Shweta Andrews
Pre-press production	Tag Response
Print production	Larissa Frost

Thanks to Jessica Cole, Lucy Doncaster, Dan Tucker

Lonely Planet offices

AUSTRALIA
90 Maribyrnong St, Footscray, Victoria, 3011, Australia
Phone 03 8379 8000 Email talk2us@lonelyplanet.com.au

USA
150 Linden St, Oakland, CA 94607
Phone 510 250 6400 Email info@lonelyplanet.com

UNITED KINGDOM
Media Centre, 201 Wood Lane, London W12 7TQ
Phone 020 8433 1333 Email go@lonelyplanet.co.uk

Although the authors and Lonely Planet have taken all reasonable care in preparing this book, we make no warranty about the accuracy or completeness of its content and, to the maximum extent permitted, disclaim all liability from its use.

MIX
Paper from responsible sources
FSC
www.fsc.org   FSC™ C021741

Paper in this book is certified against the Forest Stewardship Council™ standards. FSC™ promotes environmentally responsible, socially beneficial and economically viable management of the world's forests.

Andrew Z. Colvin: 17cla.

Corp2365, NOAA Corps Collection: 106bg.

De-benutzer-HPH: 119trb

European Space Agency: 28cl, 29tl, 56b, 128 – 129bg, 129cr, 129c; DLR/ FU Berlin/ G Neukum 66tr, 71tr, 71ca, 73tl, 76bl, 78cl, 78cla, 78ca, 78cra, 79ca, 86bc; DLR/ G Neukum (FU Berlin) et al/ Mars Express 97cr; DLR/ Mars Express f50/ G Neukum (FU Berlin) et al/ Mars Express 55ca; Foster + Partners 60 – 61t; Herschel/ PACS & SPIRE Consortium/ O. Krause/ HSC/ H. Linz 19cra; Herschel/ PACS/ L. Decin et al. 19cl; Hubble/ NASA 18cra; JAXA 78br; MPS/ DLR/ PF/ IDA 53tl; NASA/ SOHO 10bg.

European Southern Observatory: El Calcada 134cla.

Getty images: 7b, 9br, 15cr, 16cl, 16c, 16cr, 70c, 94bg, 95cr.

Indiapicture: 95tl.

Gregory H. Revera: 79tr, 122 – 123c.

iStock: 9tl, 9cr, 17cl, 18bl, 82bg, 82tr, 85c, 92 – 93t, 93tr, 98 – 99bg, 100cr, 102 – 103bg.

Jan Sandberg via Wikimedia: 8t.

Lawrence Sromovsky, University of Wisconsin-Madison/ W.W. Keck Observatory: 49cl, 58tl.

National Aeronautics and Space Administration(NASA): 10c, 16cr, 21cr, 22 – 23bg, 22cl, 23tc, 24 – 25t, 25c, 25cr, 26bg, 28cr, 28 – 29bg, 29cl, 30 – 31t, 30c, 31bc, 32bg, 34 – 35bg, 34cr, 35tl, 35tr, 35bl, 37 – 38t, 37bc, 38b, 39tcr, 39cr, 39br, 40tr, 40cl, 41tcr, 41clb, 44bl, 45tl, 46 – 47t, 46cl, 48 – 49t, 50cr, 51, 52tr, 54cb, 54cr, 55cl, 55cb, 56tr, 61tr, 80 – 81t, 81br, 96br, 99cr, 100bl, 101tr, 103tr, 110cr, 112cr, 119tl, 119tr, 119tc, 120tr, 120cr, 121c, 123tr, 124c, 124cla, 125cr, 127tl, 127bl, 128c, 129cc, 132ca, 132bc, 133cra, 133c, 133bc, 133cl, 134cr, 135tc, 136cra, 136cl, 138 – 139bg, 142 – 143t, 144cra, 145cl, 145c, 145cr, 145tr, 146cr, 146bl, 147bg, 148t, 149cr; NASA AMES 144bg; Alex Bowles 147cb; Apollo 17 crew 50 – 51b; ASTP 25bl; Caltech 108 – 109bg; Carla Cioffi 104 – 105bg, 148b;

Cassini Imaging Team/ SSI/ JPL/ ESA 57cl, 103cr; Chris Hadfield/ Roscosmos/ EPA/ YouTube/ CSA 41cr; CXC/ M. Weiss 62 – 63bg; CXC/ Stanford/ S Allen/ UC Santa Barbara/ M Bradac 58bg; ESA 76br, 109tc; ESA/ D. Aguilar (Harvard-Smithsonian Center for Astrophysics) 134 ca; ESA/ L. Roth/ SWRI/ University of Cologne 113clb; ESA/ M Wong/ I de Pater/ UC Berkeley et al 56tcr; ESA/ STScI 17tr, 52 – 53bg, 56bg; ESA/ UCSC/ Leiden University 19bg; GSFC/ Arizona State University 48br; GSFC/ TRACE 10crb; JAXA 10cla; JHUAPL 126c; John Hopkins University Applied Physics Library/ Carnegie institute of Washington 65cra, 52c; JPL 88c, 6 – 7t, 8cl, 18c, 29tr, 33c, 55crb, 57bg, 57tl, 58cr, 59t, 64tr, 65crb, 65c, 65bl, 90bg, 90cra, 90crb, 91cr, 102c; JPL USGS 69tr, 69c; JPL/ DLR 64c, 64cr, 65cr, 65crb; JPL/ SSI 57cb, 63cr, 66cr; JPL/ USGS 48 – 49c, 88bg, 91tl; JPL-Caltech 110cl, 74cl, 68bg, 74 – 75bg, 76bg, 72bg, 75bl, 132cra, 9tr, 13bg, 15bg, 60bc, 84 – 85bg, 86cr, 92c, 112bg, 125cl, 130 – 131bg, 140br, 33tr; JPL-Caltech SSI 66cl; JPL-Caltech/ ASU 110 – 111bg, 111br; JPL-Caltech/ Cornell University/ Arizona State University 18 – 19b, 54 – 55bg; JPL-Caltech/ ESA 90c; JPL-Caltech/ MSSS 54crb, 96 – 97bg; JPL-Caltech/ R. Hurt (SSC) 17ca, 19tc; JPL-Caltech/ RAP 126bg; PL-Caltech/ SSI/ G-Ugarkovic 58tr; JPL-Caltech/ T Pyle 139c; JPL-Caltech UCLA 66bg, 69bg, 101bg, 132 – 133bg, 132cl; JPL-Caltech/ USGS 67b, 116tr; JPL-Caltech/ USGS Astrology Center, Wheaton 64br, 65tbr; Ken Ulbrich 20 -21t; Lynette Cook 135cl; MSFC 22clb; SDO 10bc; Sean Smith 33br, 50tr, 65crb; Toda Strohmayer GSFC/ Dana Berry/ Chandra X-ray Observatory 139tr; World Wind 86 – 87bg.

NASA ESA C R O'Dell - Vanderbilt University: 133cla.

NASA Johnson Space Center: 20cr, 49tr, 54tr, 65tr, 71tl, 88cl, 118 – 119tc 134c, 142cr.

NASA JPL - Caltech University of Wisconsin: 61bg, 78 – 79bg, 122bg, 134 – 135bg.

NASA JPL - University of Colorado: 62cra.

NASA Planetary Photojournal: 59c.

Navicore: 73cl.

National Oceanic and Atmospheric Administration (NOAA): 85br, 109cl.

National Science Foundation: 135br.

Petar Milošević: 34cl.

Shutterstock: 114crb, 114bc.

Sir Godfrey Kneller: 27tc.

Two Micron All-Sky Survey: 17t.

Uwe Kils: 114cr.

Xavier Haubois: (Observatoire de Paris) et al via NASA 132br.